Holy Order

THE OSCOTT SERIES

General Editors
✠ Maurice Couve de Murville, Archbishop of Birmingham
Fr David McLoughlin
Fr David Evans

Oscott College was founded near Birmingham in 1794 at a time when students and staff from the English Catholic colleges abroad were being driven home by the French Revolution. In 1838 it occupied new buildings at Sutton Coldfield, built in the Gothic style, in a move which inaugurated an amibitious phase of the Catholic Revival in England. Oscott is the seminary of the Archdiocese of Birmingham which also has students from many other dioceses.

The **Oscott Series** aims at continuing the role of Oscott as an intellectual and spiritual centre of English Catholicism for close on two hundred years.

Other titles in the series are:

1. **The Unsealed Fountain:**
   Essays on the Christian Spiritual Tradition
   ✠ Maurice Couve de Murville (ed.)

2. **Niels Stensen:**
   Scientist and Saint
   Erik Kennet Pålsson

3. **Secret Hiding Places**
   Michael Hodgetts

4. **Reapers of the Harvest:**
   The Redemptorists in Great Britain and Ireland 1843-1898
   John Sharp

Aidan Nichols OP

Holy Order

The Apostolic Ministry from the New Testament to the Second Vatican Council

Oscott 5

VERITAS

First published 1990 by
Veritas Publications
7-8 Lower Abbey Street
Dublin 1

ISBN 1 85390 175 X

Nihil Obstat
Thomas Norris
Censor deputatis

The author and publishers are grateful to the following for permission to reproduce their copyright permission:
Geoffrey Chapman, a division of Cassell Publishers plc for D.N. Power OMI, *Ministers of Christ and his Church* and R.E. Brown SS, *Priest and Bishop*; St Paul Publications, Slough, and Crossroad Publishing Co. for J.M. Lustiger, *Dare to Believe*; *Priests and People* for R.J. Barret, 'Rediscovering the Diaconate' (Nov. 1988) and R. Cholij, 'Celibacy: A Tradition of the "Esteem Churches" ' (July/Aug. 1988). Augsburg Fortress Publishers for R.W. Jenson, *The Triune Identity: God According to the Gospel* and S. Terrien, *Till the Heart Sings: A Biblical Theology of Manhood and Womanhood*; Franciscan Herald Press for B. Kloppenburg, *The Priest: Living Instrument and Minister of Christ the Eternal Priest*; The *Irish Theological Quarterly* for S. Ryan, '*Episcopal Consecration: the Fulness of Order*' ITQ XXXII. Extracts from the *Revised Standard Version* of the Bible, copyright 1946, 1952, 1971 by the Division of Christian Education of the National Council of the Churches of Christ in the USA.

While every effort has been made to contact and obtain permission from holders of copyright, if any involuntary infringement of copyright has occurred, sincere apologies are offered and the owner of such copyright is requested to contact the publisher.

The cover illustration is an ordination card designed by Eric Gill for his friend Desmond Chute. It is reproduced here by kind permission of the Gill estate, from Christopher Skelton's *The Engravings of Eric Gill* (The September Press, Wellingborough, 1987). Christopher Skelton's assistance is gratefully acknowledged. The Latin inscription means 'Look whose ministry it is that is handed on to you'.

Cover design by Banahan McManus
Typesetting by Printset & Design Ltd, Dublin
Printed in the Republic of Ireland by The Leinster Leader Ltd

The fair form of Christianity rose up
and grew and expanded like a beautiful
pageant from north to south; it was
majestic, it was solemn, it was bright,
it was beautiful and pleasant, it was
soothing to the griefs, it was indulgent
to the hopes of man; it was at once a
teaching and a worship; it had a dogma, a
mystery, a ritual of its own; it had
an hierarchical form. A brotherhood of
holy pastors, with mitre and crosier and
uplifted hand, walked forth and blessed
and ruled a joyful people.

J.H. Newman, 'Christ upon the Waters':
a sermon preached in St Chad's, Birmingham,
on the occasion of the installation of the first
bishop of the see, 27 October 1850

Abbreviations

DS   H. Denzinger–A. Schönmetzer, S. J. (eds.),
*Enchiridion Symbolorum, Definitionum et Declarationum
de rebus Fidei et Morum* (Freiburg 1965 [23])

PG   *Patrologia Graeca,* ed. J.-P. Migne (Paris 1857–1866)

PL   *Patrologia Latina,* ed. J.-P. Migne, (Paris 1841–1864)

Contents

Foreword

Every candidate for the ordained priesthood is required to have a thorough knowledge of the theology of the priesthood as well as an understanding of the work, service or ministry which the priest is called upon to render to the Church. Absorbed in the mystery of Christ, offering himself with Christ as a sacrifice of love to the Father, and putting himself at the service of the people of God, the priest has special duties in the preaching of the Word, the administration of the sacraments and the pastoral care of the people.

Rapid developments in society, in the Church and in theology have brought about a certain confusion about the priesthood. The re-emphasis of Vatican Council II on the *priesthood of all the faithful,* and a growing and broadening concept of *ministry* in general have obscured in the minds of some people the distinctive features of the *ordained priesthood.* In *Holy Order* Fr Aidan Nichols OP is an excellent guide to the theology of the priesthood. The book exemplifies the theological method recommended by the Council in its Decree on Priestly Formation, *Optatam totius,* which insists that theological studies be biblically based, historically developed and magisterially sound. Fr Nichols' book is particularly lucid, learned, elegant and readable. I warmly recommend it to all priests and to all students for the priesthood.

The book was first delivered as a series of lectures in St Mary's College, Oscott, the major seminary of the Archdiocese of Birmingham, England, which has an excellent reputation for producing dedicated and pastorally competent priests, which it could not do if it did not offer a theological formation based on sound scholarship. This book is clearly part of that great tradition.

✠ William Cardinal Baum
Prefect
Congregation for Catholic Education
The Vatican
4 August 1989
*Memorial of St John Vianney
Curé of Ars*

Preface

This book originated in a course on the priesthood — the presbyterate — given at Oscott College, the seminary of the archdiocese of Birmingham. But I soon found that, in studying that particular 'holy order', it is impossible to avoid consideration of those which precede and follow in what the sixth-century Syrian Doctor who worked under the pseudonym of Denys the Areopagite called the 'ecclesiastical hierarchy'. The priesthood cannot be approached in isolation from the episcopate and the diaconate, since 'these three are one': the single sacrament of Order is triune in structure.

To the ordinary Catholic Christian, the priesthood is the order with which he or she is most familiar, and, understandably so, since it is by far the most numerous order in the apostolic ministry, and bears the heat and burden of the day in most of that ministry's activity. In this sense, it is the central image of a triptych: yet the central panel cannot be appreciated without those which flank it. We need the whole picture.

It is true that, ideally, one should situate a theology of the apostolic *ministry* within a wider account of the apostolic *Church*. To continue the metaphor introduced above, the whole picture belongs within an entire gallery. Yet, as a sacrament, Order, the embodiment of the apostolic ministry in the continuing Church, has a unity and consistency of its own. If one cannot write about a sacrament without producing an entire ecclesiology one forfeits much of one's claim to a reader's patience.

There is a particular reason at the present time for concentrating attention in this way upon the threefold ministry, and notably upon its second 'grade'. Such factors as the growth of Catholic biblical studies, the increased stress on the work of the laity in the Church and ecumenical discussion about the nature of the ministry have had the unforeseen (and quite unnecessary) consequence of obscuring for many Catholics, including not a few priests, the foundation of the ministerial priesthood in the origins of the Church. I have been particularly concerned, therefore, to draw attention to the basis of the sacrament of Order in the New Testament, and the homogeneous character of the doctrinal process whereby the contemporary teaching of the Church, as found in the decrees of the Second Vatican Council, has emerged from the past. As I hope to show, the key document of the Council on the priesthood of second rank, *Presbyterorum ordinis,* is no less than a palimpsest of that story, with all its stages detectable. There are all its leitmotifs re-orchestrated in a harmonious unity.

To show the unity of this process requires, it must be said, a definite kind of approach to the New Testament and other early Christian literature. If we accept the notion of a development of doctrine, whereby some features of Catholic faith, ethics and worship are regarded as legitimate outgrowths from New Testament origins, then we commit ourselves to what may be termed a 'hermeneutic of recognition', whereby we who share the developed consciousness of the later Church come to the evidences of the earliest Church *in positive expectation of finding* the seeds from which the great tree of the *Catholica* has grown. This is not a value-free or presuppositionless enquiry, even were such things possible. It is Scripture read in Tradition. Indeed, Tradition is, for the most part, nothing other than the reading of Scripture by the Church's eyes of faith — which organs alone are fully adequate to their wondrous object.

I wish to thank Fr Thomas O'Loughlin, of Veritas Publications, for his many valuable editorial suggestions in the finalising of this manuscript, and for additional references, and timely corrections drawn from his wide-ranging scholarship. Naturally, responsibility for the overall result must remain my own.

Aidan Nichols OP
Blackfriars
Cambridge
Solemnity of the Ascension of the Lord, 1990

1

The Apostolic Ministry in the New Testament

It has been finely said that of the gifts or offices which belong 'to Our Lord as the Christ', none can be named

> 'which he did not in its degree transfer to his apostles by the communication of that Spirit, through which he himself wrought'

— though the speaker immediately added, by way of necessary qualification,

> 'one of course excepted, the one great work, which none else in the whole world could sustain, of being the atoning sacrifice for all mankind.'[1]

So John Henry Newman, whilst still an Anglican, preaching at Oxford on 14 December 1834. It was, to Newman's mind, 'evident, as soon as stated', that an apostle, or the successor of an apostle, being the 'representative of Christ', must exceed in significance all 'Ministers of religion...whom Almighty God ever commissioned':

> the only question being, whether there is reason for thinking that Christ *has,* in matter of fact, left representatives behind him....[2]

Though we shall return to Newman before this study is ended, it will suffice here to note his claim that 'Scripture enables us to determine' this question 'in the affirmative', and so begin to test it for ourselves.

The mission of the Twelve

The starting point for any account of the apostolic ministry in the New Testament must be Jesus' appointment of the Twelve. Paul refers to the special place of the Twelve in the

Church in connection with the witnesses to the Resurrection in 1 Corinthians 15; all three Synoptic Gospels describe their appointment; the Fourth Gospel takes their existence for granted — as, for example, at John 20:24 with its reference to Thomas as 'one of the Twelve'.

Writing to the Church at Corinth, Paul reminds them:

> I delivered to you as of first importance what
> I also received, that Christ died for our sins
> in accordance with the Scriptures, that he was
> buried, that he was raised on the third day
> in accordance with the Scriptures, and that
> he appeared to Cephas, then to the Twelve (1 Co 15:3-5).

This passage takes us about as far back as it is possible to go to the absolute origins of the Christian religion. In 1 Corinthians 15:3-7, Paul is not concerned to speak in his own person. Instead, he is citing a formula, a stylised piece of oral tradition, about the accredited witnesses of the Resurrection — as his technical vocabulary of 'traditioning' or passing on the deposit of faith and 'receiving' that tradition and deposit suffice to show. We can assume that Paul received this portion of tradition about Cephas and the Twelve as part and parcel of his instruction as a catechumen — within some five years, then, of the death of Jesus himself.[3]

The Synoptics are more generous with their information. The first three evangelists present the calling and appointment of the Twelve as a major feature of Jesus' ministry. By becoming an inner circle of disciples, the Twelve are initiated into the divine secret, called by Mark 'the mystery of the Kingdom' *(4:11)*. On the basis of their intimacy with the Lord Jesus, who is the bearer of the Kingdom, and their familiarity with his teaching, the Good News about the Kingdom, the Twelve receive plenary powers to act on that Kingdom's behalf.

Matthew, Mark and Luke describe this authority in three ways. First of all, Jesus entrusts to the Twelve the worship or cultus of the new Covenant. They receive the command to baptise, issued in the great Commission at the end of Matthew. And, above all, they are made the vehicles of the tradition about the institution of the Eucharist, and receive the command to celebrate it in remembrance of Jesus — for his *anamnêsis,* something stronger in biblical Greek, with its Old Testament background, than our word 'remembrance'. For the Eucharist is the cultic act whereby, in transforming the Church's gifts of bread and wine, the Holy Spirit brings the person of Christ, and the power of his saving sacrifice, into our present.

Secondly, the Twelve are given a unique teaching role. They become the accredited recipients of its message, the *kerygma,* and the representatives of the teaching Christ, so that anyone who hears the Twelve hears Jesus himself, and thereby the Father who sent him. In communicating to the Twelve some idea of their position, Jesus could take for granted the Jewish principle of *agency,* which has it that 'An agent is like the one who sends him'.[4] Although the emphasis in this description lies on the judicial function and effects of the agent, some rabbis developed the principle of agency into what has been termed a 'judicial *mysticism*', whereby the agent becomes in some manner identical with his sender.[5] There is an analogy here between the Son's relation to the Father, and the relation of the Twelve to the Son. Versions of a saying of Jesus to this effect occur in all four gospels (Mt 18:5; Mk 9:37; Lk 9:48; Jn 13:20). This relationship, then, renders the words of those commissioned by Jesus more than simply a report on a message external to themselves. Their proclamation has a 'mysteric' dimension, for it issues from the life of the God who, in Christ, has claimed them body and soul as his own. Although we shall be looking more closely at the Gospel of John in a moment, we may note here that, in that gospel, this Synoptic claim for the Twelve will be expanded, by means of the idea of divine 'indwelling'. The Father dwells in the Son, and through the Son he also indwells the inner group of disciples. In this way, their mission will prolong the primordial mission which the Son has received from the Father. The teaching activity of the Twelve, therefore, is not limited to the passing on of the doctrinal propositions which lie implicit in Jesus' words. It also includes the communication of a more intimate, experiential understanding of the person and will of Christ, and the source of that personality and design in the being and mind of the Father. The gospel tradition, remembering the sayings of the Lord in his farewell discourse to the disciples, will ascribe this capacity of the Twelve to the influence of the 'Counsellor', the Holy Spirit.

Lastly, in the Synoptic presentation, the authority of the Twelve is also a matter of power or government. The Twelve are plenipotentiaries who will rule the new Israel, the community of the Kingdom (Mt 19:28; Lk 22:28-30). Although their power is to be exercised in humility, in a spirit of service, it is a genuine governing authority, ordered to the unity of God's people and its faithfulness to his plan.

So the Twelve enjoy, in the Synoptics, a threefold office: cultic celebration; the proclamation of the Word of God; and the government of the community of Jesus' followers, those who are initiated into the worship of the new Covenant through accepting the message of the Kingdom. These three tasks correspond, of course, to the three offices ascribed in Church tradition to Christ himself.[6] The priestly office of Christ lies in his mediating the grace of the Father, grace which is, fundamentally, the person of the Holy Spirit active in a variety of ways. Christ's prophetic office consists in his teaching divine truth about our origin and destiny; about God's being and plan; and about the interrelation of those two. Lastly, Christ's pastoral or kingly office (ever since the example of David, Scripture had spoken of those two kinds of authority in similar terms) concerns the Son's request for the obedience of the human creation, so as to present it as a harmonious unity to the Father.

So much for the Synoptics. Is their account of the work and standing of the Twelve confirmed by the evidence of the Fourth Gospel? Although that gospel lacks an explicit account of the institution of the Eucharist, the evangelist takes it for granted that his readers know of that great happening at the Last Supper. It is in this presumed context that he portrays Jesus as praying that the Twelve may be consecrated as he is consecrated — that is, set apart from the world for the service of the Father, through which others will find spiritual life, truth, and unity. The French exegete André Feuillet, in an exhaustive study of John 17, has shown that the 'traditional' (some four centuries old) title for this section of the Fourth Gospel — Jesus' 'High Priestly Prayer' — is fully justified.[7] Feuillet argues that the structure of that prayer mirrors that of the Jewish liturgy for the feast of the Atonement, while its central theme — Jesus' priestly sacrifice of himself as consecrating the Twelve to continue his mission — is indebted to the Songs of the Suffering Servant in the Book of Isaiah (42:1-4; 49:1-6; 50:4-9; 52:13-53:12).

The figure of the Servant, indeed, incorporates the three offices of Christ. The Servant has elements of the prophet about him — which explains why some have thought him modelled on Jeremiah. He also has traces of the king — which makes it intelligible that others have regarded him as patterned on Judah's last independent king, Jehoiachim. But, principally, he is presented as a priestly figure. In Numbers 18, Aaron, the prototypical Jewish high priest, is told:

> You and your sons and your whole family shall bear the burden of transgression against the sanctuary.

In Isaiah 53, the Servant of Yahweh, correspondingly but also by contrast, receives a heavier task. In his suffering, he is to bear the moral wretchedness of all humankind, and not simply the ritual faults of the Jewish people. In this way, he will win healing for the whole human race. Like the Levitical priests, the Servant offers a sacrifice of expiation: not the blood of animals, but the gift of his own life. In John 17, Jesus assumes the dual function of the Servant as priest: to offer sacrifice, and, therein and thereby, to intercede for others.

The importance of this point for understanding the mission of the Twelve in John's Gospel lies in the statement of the Johannine Christ that:

> For their sake, I consecrate myself, so that they too
> may be consecrated in the truth (Jn 17:19).

The Twelve are consecrated, that is, for the new worship 'in
spirit and in truth' which Jesus has already spoken of in his
discourse with the Samaritan woman in chapter 4 of that gospel.
The worship of the new Covenant, by contrast with that of
the old, will be a perfect or definitive worship. It will conform
to the truth brought by Jesus, and be carried out in 'spirit':
that is, by virtue of a new birth through the Holy Spirit of
God. The blessings of the new Covenant thus include a new
ministerial priesthood, embodied in the Twelve who will
celebrate its worship. This priestly office of the Twelve is a
fruit of Christ's sacrifice on the Cross — a consideration which
points to its special relationship with the Eucharist as
understood by the later Church.

Pausing for a moment in the exposition of the Fourth Gospel,
this may be a suitable point at which to note how tradition
will unfold two analogies that throw light on the priestly aspect
of the mission of the Twelve. Firstly, they bear a resemblance
to the *Old Testament* priesthood which also, as Fr Raymond
Brown has noted, had its prophetic function in the teaching
of Torah, and its pastoral function in the proclamation of the
divine will through the Urim and Thummim, the sacred
lots.[8] Within the New Testament period, although not part of
the New Testament canon, it is the First Letter of Clement
that will develop this important analogy — important, that is,
for the conviction that the new Covenant of Christ brings to
its fulfilment whatever was divinely given in the old covenant
of Israel.[9]

Secondly, the priesthood of the Twelve can also be related
to the *high priesthood of Christ,* as set forth, above all, in the Letter
to the Hebrews. In that letter, Christ's mediatorship is
portrayed in terms of the heavenly intercession initiated, and,
in essence, constituted, by his Cross. The theological
significance of these two comparisons is, however, unequal.
The analogy between the ministerial priesthood of the Twelve

and the Old Testament priesthood is grounded simply in the common concept of leadership in (sacrificial) worship. The analogy between their priesthood and that of Christ is founded, by contrast, in the reality of Christ's own being: for, as the Church's theologians, and especially Thomas Aquinas, will bring out, the consecration which the apostolic ministry carries with it is nothing other than a new share in the single high priesthood of the Saviour himself. And since this sacramental consecration of the apostolic ministry derives from the primordial consecration of our Lord's own humanity in his Incarnation and Atonement, it is appropriate that the Letter to the Hebrews alludes also to Christ's other offices: the prophetic mission which makes him the 'pioneer and perfecter of our faith' (Heb 12:2), and the authoritative pastoral care whereby he is the 'great Shepherd of the sheep' (13:20).[10]

Returning, then, to the Gospel of John, chapter 17: there the ministry of the Twelve is presented as primarily priestly, by no means excludes, therefore, the ascribing to the Twelve of prophetic and pastoral functions. On the contrary, their modelling on the figure of the Servant, via the primary realisation of that figure in Jesus himself, positively requires us to acknowledge those other functions as well. Through the Twelve, the Son will communicate to the whole Church not only life everlasting, the grace of the Kingdom, but also the knowledge of the Father and the Son: a knowledge, bound up with the prophetic office, which is both a doctrinal grasp of what the Father and the Son have done for our salvation, and a mysteric, sympathetic understanding of their relation to each other and to ourselves, and so a communion with them. Finally, and related this time to the pastoral or kingly office, the Twelve are to render the community of Jesus a unity — and not just any kind of unity but one which reflects the unbreakable unity of Father and Son themselves.

The ministry of the Twelve, as set forth in John, may thus be considered primarily priestly, secondly, prophetic and thirdly, pastoral. According to Feuillet, the consecration of the Twelve to their ministry was prepared by Jesus in the incident, recorded only by John, of the Washing of the Feet. That episode is a lesson in humility which the Twelve must learn if they are to have a 'share' (a Levitical term) with the Son in the Father's work. Their consecration (Nb 18:20) is completed in the bestowal of the Spirit for the forgiveness of sins, as described in John 20:19-23 — an event sometimes called the 'Johannine Pentecost'. In close proximity to this event, Christ gives to Peter, as leader of the Twelve, the pastoral charge of the whole Church. The Good Shepherd, who laid down his life for his sheep, places them in the care of shepherds who are to act in his name (Jn 20:15-19).

Later tradition will hold, plausibly enough, that the consecration of the Twelve for their ministry, thus prepared and completed, was fundamentally given in the command to celebrate the Eucharist, made as this was in anticipation of the Lord's glorious death. For the Eucharistic liturgy is the salvational climax to which the prophetic and pastoral activity of the ministry of the Twelve is oriented.

Before leaving that ministry, one last point may be noted. A typological parallel connects Jesus' institution of the Twelve with the Old Testament appointment of twelve tribal princes — by Moses, as recorded in Numbers 1. This event of Israel's Exodus beginnings was itself a renewal of the patriarchate, the twelve patriarchs of Genesis, and its novelty must be connected with its context: the new Mosaic covenant made on Mount Sinai, and the renewed people of Israel, delivered from bondage in Egypt. Just so, Jesus' appointment of the New Testament Twelve gives them authority within his new Covenant and community. This will be highly relevant when we come to consider the origins of the Christian presbyterate.

The apostleship

From the Twelve, we must now pass on to the wider concept of the apostleship. Luke reports in his gospel (6:13) that Jesus named the Twelve 'apostles' — but this may simply be his restatement of the affirmation of Mark (3:14) that the Twelve are *apostellesthai,* to 'go missionary'. That the Twelve were thus 'apostled' or sent on mission is clear from the Resurrection appearances in all the gospels save Mark, with its (presumed) lost ending. And even in Mark's case, the ending later added to his gospel shows how incredible it seemed to early Christians that a gospel book could finish without describing the mission of the Twelve.

Soon after the Resurrection, it became clear that the Twelve could not carry the weight of all the apostolic activity required of them. And so the apostleship was extended beyond their bounds. Frère Max Thurian, the theologian of Taizé and now a priest of the Catholic Church, describes this extension of the apostleship, whose most spectacular example is Paul of Tarsus, as a 'spiritual event' in continuity with the dominical institution of the Twelve. As Thurian puts it:

> God, who desired the institution of the Church and traditional continuity in order to show his faithfulness, also desired the spiritual event and prophetic novelty to indicate his freedom. God keeps his promises but he remains free in his sovereignty.[11]

The Pauline letters give us, indeed, our best picture of how an apostle understood the apostolic ministry. In the Letter to the Romans, Paul describes his dedication to the Gospel in priestly terms, suggesting a co-inherence of the prophetic and priestly offices within the ministry:

> On some points I have written to you very boldly by way of reminder, because of the grace given me by God to be a minister *(leitourgos)* of Christ Jesus of the Gentiles in the priestly service *(hierurgein)* of the gospel of God, so that the offering of the Gentiles may be acceptable, sanctified by the Holy Spirit *(15:15-16)*.

In 1 Corinthians, Paul speaks of himself as one of the 'stewards *(oikonomoi)* of the mysteries of God' (4:1). Both he and the other apostles act, so he claims in 2 Corinthians, as 'ambassadors for Christ, God making his appeal through us' *(5:20)*.[12] This authority is a genuine pastoral power, which leads the apostle to ask for the obedience of others (cf. Ph 2:12; 1 Co 2:17; 11:34; 16:1), and even to punish disobedience (2 Co 10:6). Such authority derives from no human source, but from an apostolic office which is itself divinely created: he is, as the preamble to the Letter to the Galatians has it:

> an apostle — not from men nor through man, but through Jesus Christ and God the Father, who raised him from the dead *(1:1)*.

However, by the same token, Paul knows that his authority is vicarious: his commands are issued in the 'name' of his Lord (1 Th 4:2; 2 Th 3:6; 1 Co 1:10).

> Not that we are competent of ourselves to claim anything as coming from us; our competence is from God, who has made us competent to be ministers of a new covenant... *(2 Co 3:5-6a)*.

Set apart (Ga 7:15; Rm 1:1), called (Rm 1:1; 1 Co 1:1; Ga 1:15), and sent by God (1 Co 1:17; Ga 2:8), the bearer of the apostolic ministry must be totally dedicated to this way of life:

> Whatever gain I had, I counted as loss for the sake of Christ. Indeed, I count everything as loss because of the surpassing worth of knowing Christ Jesus my Lord... *(Ph 3:7-8a)*.

The apostle places himself wholly at his Lord's disposition — renouncing, if need be, his right to support from the community (1 Co 9:12-18; 2 Co 11:7-10; Ph 4:10-11), giving up the possibility of marriage (1 Co 7:7), and for the Gospel's sake welcoming tribulations, whether interior or exterior, thus imitating Christ (cf. 2 Co 11:17-33) and sharing in his sufferings (cf. Ph 3:10). The apostle's life becomes, in this way, the icon of the Gospel:

always carrying in the body the death of Jesus, so that the life of Jesus may also be manifested in our bodies (2 Co 4:10).

Though Paul's accents here, as everywhere, are his own, it would be a mistake to think of this self-portrait as an autobiography. Paul insists that his own ministry is no different from the ministry of 'those who were apostles before me' (Ga 1:17). As Bishop Bonaventure Kloppenburg has written:

> His constant preoccupation — it is almost an obsession — is simply to base his rights as an Apostle on a mandate from the Lord. Here we see that the apostolic Church, to which Paul must explain himself, neither knows nor admits any apostolate but the one which derives from the clearly expressed will of Jesus and is wholly dependent on him. The ministry of the Twelve, like that of Paul, is established by a choice and calling from Christ, and is a mission for Christ, in the Holy Spirit. The ministry does not have its basis in a charism, even though it is greatly helped by the gifts of the Spirit; the basis for, or roots of, the apostolate are always in the mandate of Christ himself.[13]

How was this apostleship extended? In some cases by immediate commission from God, or from the exalted Christ, as with Matthias for the one, and, for the other, Paul himself — and possibly Barnabas, to judge from the way Paul brackets Barnabas with himself in Galatians 2. In other cases, as with Silas, who replaced Barnabas as Paul's co-apostle in Acts 15, and Andronicus and Junia, mentioned as 'among the apostles' in Romans 16, the picture is not so clear. One possibility is that apostleship could be extended by association: when Paul and Barnabas went off on different missionary journeys and Paul took Silas as his companion, he thereby associated him with the authority of his own apostleship. Alternatively, it may be, as already suggested for Barnabas, that the relatively small number of people beyond the Twelve that Paul calls 'apostles' were those who, like himself, had received a commission from the risen Lord. Thus in the text of 1 Corinthians 15, already referred to in connection with the Twelve, there are in fact two parallel lines of Resurrection witnesses. One consists of Cephas and the Twelve, together with 'about five hundred brethren'; the other comprises James the Lord's cousin, and 'all the apostles' — Paul, with suitable self-deprecation, calling himself the last and least of these. The natural inference would be that they became apostles in the way that he did.

Despite the paucity of our information, certain general principles about the process of extending the office of an apostle are clear enough. First, though the apostleship went beyond the Twelve, it had to be in solidarity with the Twelve — as Paul indirectly emphasises when presenting his own credentials to his critics. Secondly, there is a distinction of first-rate importance between apostles of Christ and 'apostles' of the congregations, like the Epaphroditus described in Philippians 2:25 as 'your apostle': an 'apostle', that is, from the church at Philippi. Such men were simply messengers of the churches, commissioned to represent their communities in some particular business — and not to represent Christ himself by a mission co-extensive with a lifetime. Thirdly and finally, if an apostle be not directly commissioned by God in Christ then he must somehow derive his apostleship from direct contact with apostles who *had* been so commissioned. Such derived apostleship — if the cases of men like Barnabas or Silas meet the condition just named — would naturally characterise individuals roughly contemporary with the original apostles, and therefore close to the founding events of the Resurrection and Pentecost. We may call them 'auxiliary apostles'.

The case of auxiliary apostles must be distinguished from another category in our reconstruction of the primitive ministry, namely, those younger men, like Timothy, whose service of the apostles made them what may be termed 'apostolic delegates'. These were junior assistants who mediated the authority of an apostle, yet did not share that authority directly. As we see from the Pastoral Letters — which represent what, at any rate, was early believed about Paul's later practice — apostolic delegates belong to the declining years of the founding generation, when the apostles themselves began to face the prospect of their own deaths as events that would take place, in all probability, before the parousia of the Lord. As Thurian writes, commenting on 2 Timothy 4:

> He (Paul) might have thought that before dying he would see that appearance, that glorious day of Christ's return, but now he felt that death was near, the fight ended, and the race over; and he would have to await Christ's appearance elsewhere. All the time he expected the Lord's return in his own lifetime, the problem of the succession to the apostleship did not arise; it was enough to extend its activity thanks to fellow-workers, companions in service and in the fight. But now that he felt death was approaching, he had to think of the next stage in his apostolic ministry, which was necessary for the unity of the churches, for the faithful maintaining of the faith, for the foundation and building of new churches, and for the organisation of ministries for training God's people.[14]

The apostolic delegates, to judge by the case of Timothy, functioned as regional vicars of the apostles, acting for them over areas considerably wider than a local church yet less than the Church universal. According to the evidence of the Pastoral Letters, they had two specific tasks, over and above their general duty to imitate the apostle in his faith and charity. First, they were to be custodians, guardians, of the apostolic deposit: the truths of divine revelation contained in the apostolic preaching.

> I charge you in the presence of God and of Christ Jesus who is to judge the living and the dead, and by his Appearing and his Kingdom: preach the Word, be urgent in season and out of season, convince, rebuke, and exhort,

be unfailing in patience and in teaching. For the time is coming when people will not endure sound teaching, but having itching ears they will accumulate for themselves teachers to suit their own likings, and will turn away from listening to the truth and wander into myths. As for you, always be steady, endure suffering, do the work of an evangelist, fulfil your ministry (2 Tm 4:1-5).

Secondly, the apostolic delegates were to organise the local apostolic ministry in the particular churches: that is, they were to ordain. Thus Timothy is also charged with the provision of *episkopoi* and *diakonoi* for local communities, as also with assuring that the *presbyteroi* are suitably honoured, and that 'widows', who could perhaps, as women, help with certain tasks of the local ministry for which men were less well suited, were duly 'enrolled' (1 Tm 3:1-13; 5:17; 22:3-16).

These specifying activities of the apostolic delegates will be important to us in a moment, when we come to consider the origins of the 'monarchical' episcopate in the primitive Church. But meanwhile, let us note that Thurian, in calling the apostolic delegates the first successors to the apostles, means that they were the first to succeed in the *supra*-local apostolic ministry of priesthood, teaching and government. In this way the apostolic delegates are to be distinguished both from the auxiliary apostles who shared in (rather than succeeding to) that supra-local apostolic ministry, and from those individuals — doubtless vastly more numerous — who succeeded the apostles in priestly, doctrinal and pastoral responsibilities at the local level, i.e. *within* a local church, rather than above it or beyond it. It is to the origins of this *local* manner of sharing in the consecrated or ordained ministry that we must now turn.

The local apostolic ministry
The first local application of the apostolic ministry to be set in place was the presbyterate — the prototypes of which are, it seems, described by Luke in Acts 6:1-6. Although what Luke calls 'the Seven' were instituted as a way of resolving the tension

between the Hebrew and Hellenist sections of the Jerusalem church, and provided the Greek-speaking element in that church with its apostolically-approved leadership, it is difficult to suppose that, for Luke, their office is a merely *ad hoc* arrangement. This is so, not simply because of the symbolism of the number seven, designed, as we shall see shortly, to parallel that of twelve, the number of the founding fathers themselves. Additionally, without the prototypical Seven, the groups of presbyters which Acts will describe or refer to so often in its pages appear without explanation, unconscionably springing up in their full ministerial armour.

The Seven, so far from being limited to a ministry of charitable administration — that 'serving of tables' which would lead in time to their identification as the earliest deacons, were actively engaged in preaching, as with Stephen, or in evangelising, as with Philip. This is not to say, however, that the link which post-biblical tradition claims to see between the Seven and the later diaconate is non-existent. The Church father Irenaeus of Lyons (c.130-c.200) will be the first to claim that the Seven of Acts are the Church's earliest deacons. Although this claim was widely accepted in the subsequent theological and liturgical tradition, Irenaeus may simply be seeking an 'apostolic warranty' for the deacon — a warrant which the necessarily tacit, and therefore in a sense ambiguous, quality of Luke's typological exposition enabled him to find.[15] The element of truth in Irenaeus' contention lies in the fact that deacons embody the 'serving', 'diaconal' aspect of the local ministry — both in terms of administering the Church's goods in favour of her poor, and as a service to the apostles (later on, the bishops): something which could, of course, include preaching should that become necessary.

As Luke portrays them, the Seven, the original presbyters, are officers locally assistant to the apostleship. They are the apostles' presbyteral local auxiliaries. Luke himself, the author of that bipartite work, 'Luke-Acts', saw such a dual ministry of apostles and presbyters (or 'elders') prefigured on two occasions in earlier times. It was, he thought, anticipated both in the Old Testament and in the actions of the earthly Jesus, during his public ministry. In Numbers 11, seventy elders were appointed to assist the twelve tribal princes in governing the 'mixed multitude' of the house of Israel. Similarly, during the historic ministry of the Lord, as reported in Luke's Gospel, Jesus sent out seventy disciples on to the Samaritan mission (10:1) to supplement the activity of the Twelve in Judaea and Galilee. Analogously, in the Acts of the Apostles, now that the original seventy of Jesus' choosing have disappeared — presumably by abandoning him in the events of the Passion, the Twelve take steps to recreate their auxiliary ministry at the local level in the persons of the Seven.

The rest of the Acts of the Apostles is full of references to such local presbyteral apostolic assistants. They crop up in the Jerusalem church in Acts 13, in the Gentile churches founded by Paul and Barnabas in Acts 14; at the 'apostolic council' of Acts 15 and, in Acts 20, at the church of Ephesus, where they are addressed by Paul as shepherds of the Lord's flock. They seem to have been modelled on the colleges of elders which were a feature of Jewish life of the time at its own local centres, the synagogues.[16] Such colleges of elders were supposed to be instituted wherever a Jewish community reached a total of 120 persons. Establishing a Christian form of the Jewish eldership, especially bearing in mind Jesus' own example in sending out the Seventy, would have been, for the Twelve, an obvious move: though, as part of the Church's constitutive origins we think of it, as does the author of Acts, as not only obvious but also Spirit-guided. Of significance for the future was the custom whereby such colleges, in Judaism, possessed a collegiate head. In the Jerusalem church, where the Christian eldership, the presbyterate, was first apostolically created, the head of the college — James, the Lord's cousin or 'brother' — soon acquired enough importance to be mentioned alongside the apostles, and not merely in subordination to them (1 Co 15:7; Ga 2:9). And while in his case this dizzy rise possibly owes much to his blood-link with Jesus, his ministerial prominence is also a portent for the future. James is a proto-presbyter, a presiding presbyter, whose position heralds that of the later monarchical bishop.[17] We may be reminded here of the Church leader in the First and Second Letters of John, who designates himself as, quite simply, 'The Presbyter'.[18]

From the evidence of Acts we can see two types of local church flourishing in the primitive community. First, there are churches with resident apostolic leaders, like the church of Jerusalem at its beginnings, or the church of Antioch under Barnabas. In such churches, apostles needed assistants of some kind in their duties of cultic celebration, proclamation of the Word and governance. We may infer from the institution of the Seven, and the broader picture painted in Acts, that these assistants were normally, but not invariably, members of the presbyterate.

For there might *also* be those who helped the apostles on the basis of intellectual or spiritual gifts. The apostles could take learned associates: *didaskaloi,* 'teachers', to aid them. These would be the forerunners of the Church's divines or theologians. Again, they might have inspired associates: *prophêtai,* 'prophets', outstanding spiritual personalities, the forerunners of the later spiritual fathers and mystical doctors of the later Church — notably in the monastic movement of the patristic period. In the nature of the case, such theological (probably, in the main, exegetical) and spiritual gifts could not be produced to order. These figures, then, could play no part in establishing the apostolic succession in the local church, though, where raised up by the Spirit in his bestowal of a diversity of gifts on the local community, they could be of great assistance to the apostolic leaders in the founding and 'edifying' of such local communities. With the benefit of hindsight, looking from the vantage-point of the post-apostolic Church, we can see that their roles derived from the differentiation of the fundamental Christian life of baptism, rather than from the development of the apostolic ministry itself. We glimpse such teachers and prophets at work in the Antiochene church in Acts 13.[19]

We may take it, however, that the norm, both statistically

and theologically, in a church with resident apostolic leadership was for the apostle(s) to co-opt presbyters for the work of their ministry in local churches, as with the Jerusalem church of Acts 15. There we find the apostles taking decisions with the concurrence of the presbyters, on the occasion when the Jerusalem community had to decide whom to send as its representative to Antioch, to convey the controversial findings of the apostolic council on the much debated question of admitting still uncircumcised pagans to the New Covenant.

But secondly, and in addition to these apostolically-led local churches, there were also churches without apostolic leaders in residence. Such churches, to judge from the testimony of Acts, were uniform in their possession of presbyteral leaders instead. Such presbyters were, of course, subject to the authority of visiting apostles. Probably because their functions included not only cultic presidency and teaching but also governing, they might also be termed *episkopoi*, 'overseers' or 'guardians', as Paul does choose to term the Ephesian presbyters in Acts 20:28.

> Take heed to yourselves and to all the flock, in which the Holy Spirit has made you guardians, *episkopoi*, to feed the Church of the Lord which he obtained with his own blood.

Just as the institution of local auxiliaries to the apostles in the shape of presbyters may have been suggested by the councils of *seniores* in the Jewish synagogues, so here also the work of the Spirit in the apostolic Church did not shun pre-existing forms of religious governance. (So too are other sacraments trans-formations of natural elements and the work of human hands.) In the life of the Qumran community, described in the Dead Sea Scrolls, we find a close parallel to the idea of *episkopoi*. In the Qumran rule of life, the official who presides over the community assembly was termed '*mebaqqêr* (supervisor) of the many', while in the related Damascus Document, each community or camp has such an overseer, with a super-ordinate version of the same official for the sect as a whole. Interestingly,

22

the *mebaqqêr* of each camp is described as the shepherd of the flock tending its distressed sheep — the very same imagery which occurs in our Acts passage.[20]

In the light of the contrast between these Jewish prototypes — the synagogue elder, and the Qumran supervisor, it seems likely that not all presbyters were such supervising, guarding or ruling presbyters. *Prèsbyter* suggests one sharing in a council; *episkopos,* on the other hand, indicates a directing hand. A church like Ephesus may well have included, then, those who were no more than simple presbyters, and as such distinguished from their more potent brethren, the presbyters with *episkopê,* with governance.

Turning to Paul's letters, we find this fundamental outline, constructed with the aid of Acts, still intact. In the first place, Paul is obviously familiar with churches led by apostles assisted by Christian prophets and teachers. As he writes in 1 Corinthians 12:28-31:

> God has appointed in the Church first apostles, second prophets, third teachers....

there being an important distinction in the original text, sometimes obscured in modern translations, between these three offices, which correspond, evidently, to the first kind of ministerial structure described above — the church with a resident apostle, assisted by exegetes and spiritual directors, and those that follow.[21] The syntax of Paul's letter draws attention to the difference from the first trio of the quintet named afterwards, for the latter include persons who mediate such preternatural gifts as miracles, healing and speaking in tongues. Nevertheless, the 'helpers' and 'administrators' who complete the list may be related to the *diakonoi* and *episkopoi* soon to be found at one place, at any rate, to which Paul sent a letter, namely Philippi. Such *episkopoi* may be understood, as we shall shortly see, as presbyters with special powers of governance, *episkopê,* and their accompanying *diakonoi* as their assistants.

In general, the local leadership of the actual churches to which Paul's own correspondence is directed fits better into the second, the basically presbyteral, pattern. In 1 Thessalonians, his earliest extant letter and probably the earliest Christian document in existence, Paul appeals to the church at Thessalonica to recognise and appreciate its *proistamenoi,* those who 'preside' over it 'in the Lord' (5:12). Moreover, he exhorts these local presidents to zealous leadership of the church — a church which, at the time, was barely more than a few months old, being, as it was, the fruit of Paul's second missionary journey. The natural assumption for any reader of Acts, our fullest source for the ecclesiological practice of the early Church, is that the Thessalonian *proistamenoi* are, by another name, the presbyters — and perhaps, more specifically, presbyters with *episkopê* — so prominent in the local communities known to Luke.[22] In these matters, there is no point in multiplying categories beyond necessity. It is more elegant to suppose that people could be referred to in more than one way. By the same token, it may be added, the *hêgoumenoi,* 'leaders', mentioned in the Letter to the Hebrews at 13:7 can also be identified with the presbyters, or presbyters with *episkopê,* now familiar to us. Just so, in modern parlance, bishops and priests can be described as Church 'leaders' or, in a liturgical context, 'presidents', without any sense of strain — and certainly without anyone denying that those so denoted *are* priests or bishops at all!

Furthermore, anyone practising what I have called, in the preface to this study, a 'hermeneutic of recognition', will find this a thoroughly acceptable reading of the evidence, since it presumes that the forms of the apostolic ministry known to the post-apostolic Church have a secure foundation in the dispositions of the apostles themselves.

It is, however, crucial to the Flemish theologian Edward Schillebeeckx's case about both the origins of the ordained ministry and its future prospects that these Thessalonian 'presidents in the Lord' were leaders put forward in spontaneous fashion by their local community without reference to the apostle who simply accepted them as a *fait*

24

accompli.[23] Schillebeeckx's interpretation, however, is not so plausible to those who accept the historical value of Acts, nor to those who expect to see in the early community signs of the later doctrine and practice of the Catholic Church. But above all, in its implicit claim that the apostles considered themselves as exempt from any responsibility in fashioning the local version of their own ministry, it goes against the grain of that concern for providing accredited leaders in the community of the new Covenant which is a hallmark of the actions both of Jesus and of the Twelve. For the very existence of the Twelve points to the first, and Paul's concern for the recognition of his apostleship by the Twelve to the second, even where the evidence of Luke-Acts (and that other monument to 'Early Catholicism', the Pastoral Epistles) is temporarily laid aside.

In effect, as the French New Testament scholar Pierre Grelot has pointed out, Schillebeeckx's thesis — which itself represents a whole tendency in modern investigation of Christian origins — sunders the Gospel message from its corporate bearer, the Church. As Grelot puts it:

> To define apostolicity, we must not separate the proclamation of the Gospel from the foundation of a solidly structured Church. The foundation of local communities that are themselves the Church of God in a given place is just as much an apostolic task as is the preaching of the Gospel, and it gives an institutional face to the expansion of the faith.

And Grelot goes on to remark that Schillebeeckx

> leaves in shadow the structural aspect of these communities and their linkage, direct or indirect, to the personal envoys of the risen Christ, so as to retain, as an index of apostolicity, only 'the Gospel of reconciliation and the forgiveness of sins...(as) transmitted by the apostles'.[24]

In other words, what the apostles conveyed, in Schillebeeckx's

25

view, was the shape of the Gospel message but not the form of the Gospel community. Others will find it little credible that the apostles and their immediate collaborators, those who continued their work, could have left believing communities to organise themselves according to their own fancy without endowing them, from the beginning, with structures which should thus be termed 'apostolic'.

To highlight the probable connection between the 'presidents in the Lord' and Paul's apostolic authority, we may turn from that church in Thessalonica to its sister at Corinth. In 1 Corinthians, Paul's most problematic daughter church is faced with faction, the collapse of discipline, liturgical disorder and the abuse of charismatic gifts. Paul insists that such gifts must be seen in their wider context, within the perspective of the entire work of God in the body of Christ. As we have already noted, here stands first and foremost the apostle himself; next there is the *prophêtês* and the *didaskalos,* the 'prophet' and the 'theologian'. Again, there are those with extraordinary gifts of the kind which the Twelve manifested in the immediate aftermath of Pentecost: workers of mighty (miraculous) deeds, healers, and 'speakers in various kinds of tongues'. Sandwiched in between the last mentioned, there are also 'helpers' — those engaged in charitable activities, and those entrusted with *kubernêsis,* 'administration'. In other words, within the local church is a variety of gifts, tasks and functions which must be brought into an ordered harmony, for God 'is not a God of disorder'. Who, then, is to exercise such ordering authority? Paul tells us in 16:15-16:

> I beseech you, brethren, you know the household of Stephanas, that it is the first-fruits of Achaia, and that they set themselves to the service, *diakonia,* of the saints. I urge you to be subject to such men, and to all those who share their works and labour. I rejoice in the visit of Stephanas, of Fortunatus and Archaicus: they have made up for your absence, they have refreshed my spirit as well as yours. Show recognition to such men.

Further light is thrown on the status of Stephanas, Fortunatus, Archaicus and their assistants by the formula of address in Paul's letter to yet another community in modern-day Greece, namely, Philippi. Paul addresses his letter to 'all the saints in Christ Jesus that are at Philippi, with their *episkopoi* and *diakonoi*' (1:1). Assuming that the apostolic 'structures' given by Paul to the churches of Philippi and Corinth are cognate — both were the fruit of his second and third missionary journeys — these terms of address can illuminate the named leaders and their anonymous helpers at Corinth. Stephanas, together with his fellow-workers of comparable standing, appear to be overseers, presbyters with *episkopê,* and in this sense *episkopoi,* whilst those members of Stephanas' household co-opted as instruments of his ministry would correspond, then, to the Philippian 'deacons'. Whilst in no way claiming *episkopê,* they too had devoted themselves to the *diakonia* of the saints. Some years later, Clement of Rome, when writing to the church at Corinth, will refer to the apostolic institution of *episkopoi* and *diakonoi,* in the course of expounding the derivation of the ministry, via the apostles and, behind them, Christ himself, from God.

> Now the Gospel was given to the apostles for us by the Lord Jesus Christ; and Jesus Christ was sent from God. That is to say, Christ received his commission from God and the apostles theirs from Christ. The order of these two events was in accordance with the will of God. So thereafter, when the apostles had been given their instructions, and all their doubts had been set at rest by the resurrection of our Lord Jesus Christ from the dead, they set out in the full assurance of the Holy Spirit to proclaim the coming of God's kingdom. And as they went through the territories and townships preaching, they appointed their first converts — after testing them by the Spirit — to be bishops and deacons for the believers of the future.....[25]

Clement could of course, assume that his Corinthian readers would know whether Stephanas and his household were in fact examples of such *episkopoi* and *diakonoi* or not. Moreover, the idea that deacons were the junior relatives and servants of an *episkopos* fits in well with what we know of deacons as the ordained assistants of the bishop in the sub-apostolic Church.[26] This may be a good point to note that the deacon, unlike the presbyter and the *episkopos*, has no clear Jewish (much less pagan) archetype. The glory of his particular office lies in its growing from out of the distinctive *diakonia*-quality which the Christ communicated to the ministry of the Church he founded.[27]

But what, then, has happened to the presbyters — with whom we have earlier identified the presidents of the church at Thessalonica in such Pauline churches as Corinth and Philippi? One obvious possibility is simply that the names *presbyteroi* and *episkopoi* were interchangeable in Paul's practice, as indeed his address to the Ephesian elders in Acts 20 suggests. There is, however, another possibility which fits in a more satisfactory way the insistence of the later Church that the apostolic ministry, as she has inherited it, is 'triune': threefold in nature. It may be that, in the churches of Corinth and Philippi, the presbyteral order is comprised within the totality of the church addressed, with only the embryo bishops and deacons singled out for special mention. It is possible that, in some, at any rate, of the New Testament churches, the presbyterate was extremely numerous, being, as in Judaism, a representative selection of the older men: in the Christian case this would be, rather, the converts of longer standing. Take, for instance, the Apocalypse of John, with its glimpses of the churches of Asia Minor for whom the book was written. In 4:2-4, we hear of heavenly presbyters who stand before the throne of God.[28] These figures are either the souls of presbyters who have fallen asleep in the Lord, or, alternatively, they are the angel guardians of the Church's living presbyters. But the point to which we should attend is that they are twenty-four in number: a biblical way of saying that there is a whole host of them, twice the number of plenitude, twelve. A congregation, in fact, may have been understood as made up of elders and juniors, of a presbyteral college together with its laity. One suggestion is that much New Testament correspondence was pursued with such large bodies of presbyters who represented in a massive way their local church. In Acts 15 the letter of the Jerusalem church to its sister church at Antioch is composed in the name of the apostles and presbyters. So presumably, in a church without resident apostles, such letters would be penned in the names of the presbyters alone. Thus if, for example, in 1 Corinthians, Paul is answering a letter to himself from the Corinthian presbyters, this would explain both why he fails to talk about them and also why the Corinthian church is advised to accept the leadership of Stephanas and his immediate colleagues. A large senate of older men would not be able to secure unity of leadership in a difficult, because divided, situation. As the Anglican student of Christian origins, Austin Farrer, wrote:

> A great part of any Pauline epistle is addressed to an inner circle: this leaps to the eye.[29]

Farrer considered that Colossians, Galatians and Romans are other Pauline letters which make more sense if substantial sections of them were addressed to presbyters.

The emergence of 'embryo bishops' within a wider council of presbyters receives its clearest attestation in the Pastoral Epistles which, if not simply Pauline, may be indebted to Luke, whose presentation of the Lord's ethical teaching they echo. Though *episkopê* is not yet focused in a monarchical figure within the local church, nevertheless a descriptive term applied to all, most or many presbyters, according to circumstances, is in process of becoming a technical term reserved to their head, as the one steward and father of the Christian community, itself likened, in a pervasive metaphor of those letters, to a household or family.[29]

And so the New Testament evidence, fragmentary as it is, suggests the beginning of a threefold ministry of presidency in the local churches. This local ministry is established by reference to apostolic authority, though as yet, within the New Testament, it does not actually inherit that authority in its universal form. Within the New Testament corpus, the chief

overall contrast is that between the universal apostolic ministry
— the Twelve, the wider apostleship, the auxiliary apostles
and apostolic delegates — and the local ministry of presbyters,
presbyters with *episkopê* or overseers and deacons. Since this
is the dominant contrast, it is predictable that the authors of
the material will tend to telescope the local ministries, and
notably those of presbyter and overseer. Only later, when the
apostles have disappeared from the scene will the distinction
between eldership and *episkopê* be expressed as a difference in
order. Though all the ordained ministers in the New Testament
churches enjoyed their authority by reference to the authority
of the apostolic founders, the apostles did not simply hand over
their total mission as rulers, teachers and celebrants of Christian
worship to those presbyteral leaders who were the dominant
form of local ministry in the wake of the institution of the Seven
in the mother church, Jerusalem. Something which the
presbyters lacked, those with *episkopê* will eventually attain.
In attaining it, the bishops, as they will be known, will
precipitate a re-alignment of the three chief forms which the
local apostolic ministry took. But whereas this re-alignment
will not greatly modify the character of the diaconate, except
perhaps to reinforce its intimate dependence on those possessed
of *episkopê*, the presbyterate will emerge in much different form
— for though historically it is the immediate origin of the
episcopate it will come to be, first theologically and practically,
and eventually doctrinally, in subordination to it.

The precise stages in the full takeover of universal apostolic
authority by the local ministerial leadership cannot now be
traced. What we may say is that the process could not be
completed until the local ministerial authority had been
rendered a suitable vehicle for it. It needed to become at once
more personal and more unified, more a matter of responsible
commission and more a matter, too, of serving to focus the
wider Church and ministry. It became a suitable vehicle for
the full universal apostolic ministry with its concentration in
a single head, the mon-*episkopos* or monarchical bishop. The
emergence of single episcopal leaders of the presbyteral colleges

of local churches, episcopal leaders assisted by their deacons, created a vehicle capable of carrying apostolicity — such full apostolic authority as is needful for carrying out the intentions of the Lord Jesus in worship, teaching and governance throughout the universal, as well as the local church, when the apostles themselves, and their auxiliaries and delegates, had finally gone.

Summary and doctrinal conclusion

In the apostles, the Lord Jesus left to his community a ministry, for the purposes of sanctifying, teaching and governing it. The apostles are to preside over the worship that belongs to the new Covenant, and especially its Eucharistic meal-sacrifice they are to proclaim the Word as Jesus' envoys; and they are to provide discipline for the community, to rule the new Israel. Such a summary of what apostles are for is arrived at by grouping together material about the Twelve, on the one hand, and about the apostleship in general on the other. But that procedure is fully legitimate. For the New Testament, all apostles are in solidarity with the mission of the original Twelve.

In the communities which they founded, the apostles established local community leaders. Sometimes, these leaders are referred to in large terms, as *hêgoumenoi,* 'leaders', or *proistamenoi en tô Kuriô,* 'presidents in the Lord'. More frequently, however, they are called *presbuteroi, episkopoi* and *diakonoi.* The difference between *presbuteros* and *episkopos* is not clear-cut. Most probably, churches without apostolic leaders in residence were governed by colleges of presbyters, some of whom had concentrated responsibility. This inner circle possessed *episkopê:* oversight or supervision of the entire presbyterium and (thereby) of the whole local church. Non-episcopal presbyters differed from deacons in that the former enjoyed an active share in organising Church life, whilst the latter were rather instruments of the *episkopoi.*

The New Testament contains, then, the beginnings of the threefold ministry. Such ministers were mandated by the apostolic founders who (presumably) recognised in them gifts of the Spirit, as of nature, equipping them for the task in hand. That task can only be conceived of as a local application of the task of the apostles themselves. That is, it consisted in presidency in worship, teaching and the exercise of discipline. Though the texts do not describe this ministry in its day-to-day action, the manner and the rationale of its introduction, notably in the Lucan Seven, allow no other reasonable inference. But nowhere in the New Testament is it suggested that these local ministries enjoy the full universal ministerial authority of the apostles themselves. In so far as anyone other than an apostle has authority over the churches at large, as distinct from an authoritative position within a church, this would be an 'apostolic delegate' of the kind exemplified in Timothy or Titus: younger contemporaries of the apostles, seen in the Pastoral Letters making provision for local ministries within a region, on behalf of the apostle Paul.

On the other hand — and this is a point of some doctrinal importance, the local ordained ministry would not be, properly speaking, sacramental, a sacramental reality in its own right, unless it originated in the same action whereby Jesus Christ himself instituted the apostolate as an effective sign of his continuing authority in the Church. This crucial point, raised today by such critical theologians as Hans Küng and Edward Schillebeeckx, as by the contributors to the multi-authored volume, *Le ministère et les ministères selon le Nouveau Testament* (1974), was already debated at the start of this century, during the intensive enquiry into Christian origins which preceded and sparked off the Modernist crisis. The central issue was summarised in advance in proposition fifty of the decree of Pius X's Holy Office, *Lamentabili,* in 1907. That proposition, which is a précis of the position the papacy of that period proposed to combat, reads:

> The *seniores* encharged with supervising Christian assemblies *(invigilandi munere)* were instituted by the apostles as presbyters *(presbyteri)* or bishops *(episcopi)* so

as to provide for the good order necessary in constantly growing communities, but not, properly speaking, in order to perpetuate the apostolic mission and authority itself. (DS, 3450)

Naturally, a document such as *Lamentabili* is, by itself, insufficiently weighty to constitute a final resolution of a disputed question in Christian doctrine. Yet in this case its framers were right to see this thesis, apparently innocuous as it is, as a body-blow to the Catholic concept of Church and ministry alike. For, if the ordained ministry were brought into being by the apostles simply as something useful for the local church but wholly distinct from their own calling — a quite separate office not intended to apply, or to inherit, the apostolic ministry itself, then Order is merely a matter of organisational convenience in the Church and not a sacramental reality in its own right. Order ceases then to be a covenanted gift of the Father, made through the economies of the Son and the Spirit for the mediation of the divine reality — as spiritual life (the priestly office), transcendent truth (the prophetic office) and all-embracing unity (the pastoral office) in the community of the new Covenant.

What we should say is, rather, that the apostles, in instituting local ordained ministries for the good order of the communities they had founded, necessarily conceived such ministry as involving good order in cultic presidency, teaching and pastoral discipline, since these are the constitutive dimensions of the Church's common life. Thus, the local ordained ministry they set in place was an application of their own apostolic ministry. Furthermore, and in dependence on the gradually developing conviction of the delay of the Parousia, this was not simply a question of arrangements made necessary by the fact that the apostles could not be everywhere at once. It was also a matter of taking steps that could lead the apostolic ministry with its mission, to pass into the ordained ministry, if and when the disappearance by death of all the apostles, and their assistants, the 'apostolic men', should take place.

The New Testament age, then, hands on to the future the idea of the apostolic ministry, and, more than the idea, the reality, as that is constituted by Jesus Christ, and, through the operation of his Spirit, by the inspired apostolic heads of the earliest community in fidelity to their Master's plan and will. The conviction that the ordained ministry is sacramentally rooted in the ministry of the apostles, that it is, indeed, that same ministry, in so far as the latter is transmissible through time, will remain for the future — and not least at the Second Vatican Council of the mid-twentieth century — the fundamental affirmation of the Catholic Church where the sacrament of Order is concerned.

2

The Age of the Fathers

We ended our review of the New Testament community by invoking the notion of 'apostolic succession': the inheritance, by the local ordained ministry, of the ministry of the apostles (and thus of the Twelve) themselves. This was a theme which, as we shall see, played an important role in thinking about the ministry in the post-apostolic period. We must turn now to the sub-apostolic, or early patristic, development of the New Testament origins. The period covered by these 'early patristic' developments may be defined as beginning with the earliest post-New Testament writers and continuing up to the Council of Nicaea in 325. So we will be looking first of all at the pre-Nicene, or ante-Nicene, community, and only subsequently at developments after Nicaea. In each of these two periods, at once divided and joined by that great Council, we shall, so far as possible, separate out what the sources have to say about bishops, about presbyters and about deacons, in that sequence.

The ministry in the ante-Nicene Church
First, then, the place of the bishop of the pre-Nicene Church. In the mid to late second century, the sources are interested in the episcopal ministry — still not, in some cases, fully distinguished, at least terminologically, from the ministry of presbyters with *episkopê* — primarily because they are interested in what counts as apostolic teaching over against heresy.[1] By way of reaction against the claim of the Gnostic heresiarchs, like Basilides and Valentinus, to have inherited a secret tradition of teaching stemming from the apostles, orthodox or mainstream writers claim that the teaching office of the apostles, in point of fact, has been inherited by the *episkopoi* (Latin, *episcopi*) in the churches founded by the apostles, and in other churches in communion with those so founded. Thus Irenaeus of Lyons,

writing around the year 180 in his treatise *Against the Heresies,* remarks:

> We ought to listen to those presbyters of the Church who have the succession from the apostles....who, with the succession of the episcopate, have, by the Father's good pleasure, received the infallible *(certum)* charism of truth.

And Irenaeus goes on to say that, by contrast with the Christian authority of these episcopal presbyters,

> others who are outside the original succession, and hold their meetings in holes and corners, we must treat with suspicion.[2]

In other words: over against the ordained successors of the apostles are the private meetings of unauthorised Gnostic teachers with their personal followings in their own lecture-rooms. For Irenaeus, the sacramental *charisma,* 'grace', received in episcopal ordination is a guarantee of authenticity of apostolic teaching, and such assurance of the continuing self-identity of the Gospel message can be secured by no other means. This same idea of the succession of the *episkopoi* to the teaching office of the apostles is echoed in other second-century authors such as Hegesippus, and (in his Catholic period) Tertullian.[3]

But, if the bishops had thus inherited the ministry of the apostles — ultimately, of the Twelve, then teaching could not, of course, be their only function. The prophetic office of the Twelve is inseparable, as we have seen, from their priestly and kingly offices. And indeed, if we turn to the third century, when the troubles of the Church were concentrated more on schism than on heresy, the emphasis is placed on the liturgical (priestly) and pastoral (kingly) functions of the bishop — somewhat to the exclusion of his teaching office or *didaskalia (magisterium).* In the third-century sources, the bishop is described characteristically as the high priest (his liturgical role) and the shepherd (his pastoral role) of the local church. As high priest, the bishop baptises and confirms new laics (lay-people), ordains new clerics, and offers the holy Gifts, assisted by his laity and clergy, at the Eucharist. As pastor, he unites the whole local church to itself by uniting its members to his own person. He also unites it to other local churches elsewhere in the single communion of the (in principle) world-wide Catholic Church.

Thus, for instance, in Cyprian, the bishop is not, as for Irenaeus, a teacher but, rather, *sacerdos,* a high-priest. This is the normal term for a bishop, not only in Cyprian's letters but in those of other people to him. At the same time, in his treatise *On the Unity of the Church,* Cyprian set forth what would become the classic statement of the bishop's unitive role, exercised in pastoral discipline, *vis-à-vis* his own laity and clergy within the local churches, but in relation also to the other bishops — and so to *their* local churches as well. It is, in Cyprian's view, through the solidarity of the entire episcopate that the whole Church is united to itself, in reflection of the unique unity of Father, Son and Holy Spirit as the one God. Cyprian's book, in fact, might well have been entitled *On the Bishops.*

So far I have been drawing attention to the writings of some *individual* figures within the ante-Nicene community. If we turn from such texts to their anonymous and yet more fully common or public counterparts, namely, the *liturgical* sources of the pre-Nicene age, we find the emerging pattern generally confirmed — except, perhaps, in one striking particular. Investigation of the early ordination rites suggests that the third-century stress on the bishop as liturgist ('presider at the rites of worship') or high-priest and as pastor or 'uniter' may have been a reversion to an earlier, indeed the earliest, post-New Testament understanding of his ministry. The Liturgy, conservative by essence as it is, may preserve a configuration which the development of doctrine, or of theology, has elsewhere caused to change. Thus the emphasis on the bishop's *priestly* and *pastoral* offices seems, in the light of the prayer for his consecration which we shall be looking at in a moment, to be something of a reversion to the state of affairs in the early second century — before the Gnostic crisis, whose own dates are c. 130 to c. 180, had highlighted the *teaching* aspect of the

37

bishop's ministry.

In the earliest known ordination prayers, found in Hippolytus of Rome's treatise *The Apostolic Tradition* — a work which is itself self-consciously conservative and perhaps even deliberately archaising, what we hear of are the governing and liturgical functions which the episcopal candidate is to acquire. More specifically, the consecrating bishop asks for the descent of the Holy Spirit on to the candidate under the title of *to hêgêmonikon Pneuma,* the 'governing Spirit', whom, so the prayer maintains, the Father gave to Christ, and Christ gave to his apostles.

> Grant it...to this your servant
> whom you have chosen for the episcopate,
> to shepherd your holy flock,
> to serve you as your high-priest, blamelessly
> ministering night and day, ceaselessly to
> propitiate your countenance, offering to you
> the gifts of your holy Church.

Mention of these liturgical functions, which belong more properly to the bishop's priestly office than to his pastoral one, then leads the prayer to speak of the Holy Spirit under a second title, namely, as *to archieratikon Pneuma,* and to round off its account of the bishop's liturgical duties by reference to his role in sacramental penance, in ordination, and in the acceptance or rejection of others from the Church's eucharistic communion:

> By the high-priestly Spirit may he
> have authority to forgive sins according to your
>   command,
> to ordain according to your bidding,
> to loose every bond, according to the authority
> which you gave to the apostles.[4]

In this earliest known prayer of episcopal consecration, the bishop's office, as already mentioned, is essentially twofold, governing and sanctifying, with his teaching work left in shadow. But it may also be noted that this twofold office reflects a *further* twofoldness in the bishop's position. He is presented as a middleman between God and the Church, and between the Church and God. In the first part of the ordination prayer, there is a parallelism between the pastoral office, in which the bishop represents God, the divine shepherd, to the Church, God's flock, and the priestly office, by which he represents holy Church to the Father, sharing in Christ's office of high-priest which belongs to the Mediator in his humanity. His pastoral or governing role presents him as a divine representative to the Church; his liturgical role, as principal offerer of the Church's eucharistic sacrifice, makes him the human representative of Christ's Church.

These convictions of the Church in Hippolytus' time are reflected in later second- and third-century writers, especially when liturgical sources are likely to be in their minds, for instance by Tertullian in his treatise *On Baptism* and in Cyprian's letters.[5] Moreover, the text we have been following, the *Apostolic Tradition,* claims to describe not only the traditional practice of the Roman church, over against the innovations of Hippolytus' papal opponents, but the traditional practice of the churches everywhere. The fact that his book was widely adopted in the Christian East, and exists in Syriac and Coptic as well as Greek, suggests that his claim was not without foundation. His conviction that the bishop was the high-priest and pastor *par excellence* of the local church received independent confirmation in, for Egypt, the *Sacramentary* of Sarapion[6] (d.c.360), and, for the Syriac-speaking churches, the *Didascalia Apostolorum.*[7]

In its portrait of the bishop, the *Apostolic Tradition* harks back unwittingly — or, if wittingly then silently — to perhaps our earliest post-New Testament sources in study of the ordained ministry, namely, the Letters of Ignatius of Antioch. For Ignatius, the bishop is essentially the unifier of the local church as celebrant of its mystical banquet in the Eucharistic assembly.[8] In other words, he is the anticipation of Cyprian's *pastor* and *high priest.* So far from drawing his readers' attention to the teaching office of the bishop, Ignatius praises him for his silence which, symbolically, links him to the absolute Origin, the Father, from whom the Word, Jesus Christ, proceeds.[9] Around the bishop all must gather, uniting themselves to him in full obedience, doing nothing without him. To be with the bishop is to have a part in the Church, and so in Jesus Christ, and so in God. Whereas not to be with him, as the dissidents and false doctors are not with him, is to lack all these realities.[10] For Ignatius, the bishop represents, indeed, either Christ or the Father himself;[11] it is the presbyteral college which, in his eyes, mirrors the role of the apostles in the Church.[12] This would seem to imply that in Ignatius' church it is the presbyters who do the active instruction — although, of course, his own letters are, paradoxically, examples of a teaching bishop in action.

And just as, in this way, the sub-apostolic bishop is acting as a teacher, whether he speaks of himself as one or not, so in the later ante-Nicene period the episcopate was far from forgetting its teaching office, despite the passing of the Gnostic threat to the apostolic faith. A number of the homilies of ante-Nicene bishops have come down to us, such as, for example, that of Melito of Sardis (d.c.190) *On the Pasch*. And these can be supplemented by episcopal literary activity in other forms: the letter, or the treatise. And increasingly, the bishops were getting together in councils, at least on a regional basis, to act as judges of the Church's faith. It is such periodic re-convokings of the episcopal college, stimulated first by the movement 'Away from the Old Testament!' which we call Marcionitism, and then by the Trinitarian and Christological heresies of the age, that — more than anything else — testifies to how widespread was the bishops' conviction that they had succeeded to the role of the apostles in the Church. Awareness of this office allowed patristic writers to link episcopal consecration with the descent of the Spirit, in wind and flame, at Pentecost. Thus Severian of Gabbala, in a homily on Whitsun, of which fragments are preserved in the exegetical *catenae* ('chains' of citations) on the Acts of the Apostles:

Why did the apostles receive the tongues of fire on their heads? Because they were ordained as teachers of the whole world; now ordination is never performed save on the head. The coming down of tongues on the head is, therefore, the sign of an ordination. In fact, it is on the head that ordination takes place, as the custom has been maintained even to our own days. For, since the coming down of the Holy Spirit is invisible, on the head of him who is to be ordained high priest (bishop) is laid the book of the Gospel; and in this book thus laid must be seen naught else save a tongue of fire; a tongue because of the preaching of the Gospel, and a tongue of fire because it is said, 'It is fire that I have come to spread over the earth'.[13]

The grace of the fullness of Order, then, is here described in Pentecostal terms, as light and strength, given to the bishops to make them witnesses, bearers of the apostolic word, and unerring guides of the people of God.[14]

What we are seeing, then, in the pre-Nicene episcopate is the gradual dawning of the consciousness that the bishops had inherited the apostolic ministry in its three essential dimensions: the priestly, the prophetic, the pastoral — even though the rate at which that awakening took place for any one of these offices may have varied as now one, now another took on the greater importance for the communication of the Gospel in the Church.

So much for the bishop in the pre-Nicene community; but what of the presbyter and the deacon? In Hippolytus' ordination ritual, the presbyter's tasks are mainly to govern and, following Dom Gregory Dix's reconstruction of the original text in the light of its Coptic derivative — to teach.[15] But he also receives a share in the liturgical functions of the bishop. The presbyter joins in the imposition of hands on a new presbyter (but not on a deacon), and in the consecration of the elements at the Eucharist. Fifty years later, in the time of Cyprian, the presbyter is found presiding at the Eucharist, either alone or together with other presbyters.[16] This was a

41

practice early anticipated, since it is presumably the presbyters that Ignatius has in mind when he writes

> Let that be considered a valid Eucharist which is celebrated by the bishop, or *by one whom he appoints*.[17]

The deacon of Hippolytus, by contrast, is explicitly said to be ordained 'not for priesthood, but for the service of the bishop'. He does not receive the 'common spirit of the presbyterium' (the word 'spirit' here should, perhaps, be capitalised, as a reference to the *Holy* Spirit), but rather what is 'entrusted to him by the bishop's power'.[18]

In the pre-Nicene age it is sometimes difficult to distinguish the special liturgical functions of the presbyter from those of the bishop above him or, again, from the deacon below. For it is assumed that all three orders are present together. This collaborative co-presence of the three orders is beautifully brought out in Ignatius' letters, where it forms part of an exhortation to preserve unity around the threefold ministry:

> I exhort you to strive to do all things in harmony with God: the bishop is to preside in the place of God, while the presbyters are to function as the council of the Apostles, and the deacons, who are most dear to me, are entrusted with the ministry of Jesus Christ, who before time began was with the Father and has at last appeared. Conform yourselves, then — all of you — to God's ways, and respect one another, and let no one regard his neighbour with the eyes of the flesh, but love one another at all times in Jesus Christ. Let there be nothing among you tending to divide you, but be united with the bishop and those who preside — serving at once as a pattern and as a lesson of
> incorruptibility.[19]

But the general principle would seem to be that the deacon, being only the liturgical assistant of the bishop, cannot act by himself: above all, at the Eucharist. When, during the Great

Persecution under Diocletian and his successors at the start of
the fourth century, some deacons took it upon themselves to
celebrate the Eucharist in the absence of bishop or presbyter,
they were at once rebuked for this by the Western councils
of Elvira (c.306) and Arles (314). The presbyter, by contrast,
has no special liturgical office when the bishop is present. But
in the absence of the bishop, the presbyter, unlike the deacon,
can act as his liturgical deputy and perform his sacramental
functions, assisted by the deacon.

The exceptions to this rule — that the presbyter can do what
the bishop does when the bishop is not there — concern
confirmation and ordination itself. The presbyter would never
inherit the bishop's role as ordainer (except in the participating
sense already mentioned, or by way of abuse). This was so for
reasons whose significance we shall look at in a moment. But
for the time being we can note that it is no coincidence that
the two sacramental tasks which fell exclusively to the bishop
were confirming and ordaining. Both kinds of sacramental act
are ecclesially creative, in that they entail initiating candidates
into one or other of the two kinds of mediation of Jesus Christ's
high-priesthood which make the Church his priestly people.
Confirmation is the induction of the baptised into the full status
of members of the *laos* — the royal and universal priesthood
of all believers. It creates new 'laics', and as such parallels the
creation of new 'clerics' — the induction of the confirmed into
the distinctive, additional share in Christ's headship which is
the ordained ministry. Confirming and ordaining confer on
new candidates the mission of the Church herself. This mission,
initiated in the divine life, mediated by Christ and passed on
through the apostles, exists either in a general lay form, or in
a special ordained one, in service of the whole body. Only the
bishop, the plenary bearer of the apostolic ministry, was the
appropriate person to pass on the mission charge, and the
consecration it required — by virtue of what Hippolytus had
called the 'high-priestly Spirit' conferred on the apostles, and
on the bishops after them.

43

If, despite this explanation, the reader feels that the distinction between the constituent parts of the threefold ministry and especially between presbyter and bishop, was not as clear in the pre-Nicene Church as he or she might like, there is comfort in the fact that Dix, that great Anglican historian of the Liturgy and defender of the Catholic doctrine of ministerial Order thought so as well. In his essay 'The Ministry in the Early Church', Dix refers to what he calls 'a curious lack of adjustment' between the offices of bishop and presbyter in the period before Nicaea. As he summed up:

> The episcopate was something wholly distinct from the presbyterate, yet the bishop could be called a 'presbyter' with perfect courtesy and called himself so. The presbyter can at need perform almost all the sacramental functions which are the bishop's special prerogative (even having a part in the ordination of presbyters), yet the bishop actually does rule and teach the Church, which was theoretically the special function of the presbyters.[20]

The most economical explanation for this state of affairs, as well as the one best befitting developed Catholic doctrine, takes us back to the distinction which has been with us from the very start of our investigation: namely, the difference between the full, universal apostolic ministry and its partial, local application. In the New Testament Church, the local ministry was not something entirely distinct from the apostolic ministry, but neither was it simply identical with that ministry. As we have seen, a figure like Timothy was a kind of go-between linking the apostleship with the apostolically derived structures of the local ordained ministry. In the generation after the age of such apostolic delegates, however, or so I wish — following Dix — to argue, the apostleship, in so far as it was communicable beyond the founders of the Church themselves, merged with the local ministry. Or, to put it better, the local ministry came to inherit the full authority of the apostolic ministry.

This merger, inheritance or 'adjustment' of the apostleship to the local ministry, which can be dated to approximately the years 100-150, caused the bishop to have a composite office. In the first place, he derived his special liturgical functions in his own church from that ministry which was summed up in the figure of James, the Lord's 'brother', in the Jerusalem church — the ministry of a supervising or proto-presbyter, a 'first' presbyter who would be the natural choice when a minister was needed to 'give thanks' *(eucharistein)* at the Eucharist, acting in the person of Christ at the Last Supper.[21] Because of the connection between the later bishop and the proto-presbyter in this priestly aspect of the ordained ministry, the proto-presbyter is sometimes referred to by modern students of this subject as the 'primitive *episkopos*'. Secondly, the pre-Nicene bishop derived his pastoral functions from his presidency of the local presbyterate, which remained closely associated with him in its exercise. But thirdly, and here is the factor which makes the bishop unique: his special responsibility for orthodoxy of doctrine in the Church (as expressed, say, in Irenaeus) and his power of ordination (as described in, for instance, Hippolytus) were inherited from the apostolic delegates who exercised precisely these two functions — guarding the doctrinal deposit and ordaining local ministers — at the close of the New Testament period, as the Pastoral Letters show us. These latter functions — guarding doctrine and appointing 'presidents in the Lord' for local churches— may be considered as attributes of the full universal apostolic ministry, aspects of the commissions of the original apostles. Such authority over the faith and life of the Church implies powers of the fullest kind — plenipotentiary powers. It implies, in fact, the kind of powers Christ had given to the Twelve. Such powers could not be generally transferred to the local ministry on the deaths of the original apostles. Why so? Because the 'corporate' type of presbyteral ministerial organisation had not yet developed a sufficiently clear personal organ to which the full apostolic commission could be transferred — even though presbyteries were beginning to develop such an organ in some places, where *episkopê* was concentrated not just in the hands of few, as at Corinth in the time of Paul, but into the hands of a single person, as in the Syrian and Asiatic churches so helpfully described by Ignatius of Antioch around the year 110. As this 'monepiscopal' type of presbytery and church became ever more universal, so the 'adjustment' of the apostolate to the local ministry took place. In other words, the bishops became, through their consecration, in full reality, the successors of the apostles.

What, then, of the presbyters? Their office, although it was the most ancient local ordained ministry in the Church — the original local ordained ministry, that of the Seven — could not be unaffected by the merger of the two main kinds of apostolic ministry, universal and local, in the persons of the bishops. As a result of the establishment of the apostolic succession as we know it, the presbyterate was re-aligned with that dramatic, yet peaceful revolution. It now defined itself in terms of a share in the bishop's ministry, just as once upon a time, in the Acts of the Apostles, it had defined itself in terms of its relationship to the apostles themselves. From now on, presbyters would belong to the apostolic succession only through their ordination by bishops who embodied that succession. By thus sharing in the succession, albeit via the bishops, they will inevitably also share in the threefold ministerial office of priesthood, teaching and government, not just locally as hitherto but, in principle at any rate, on the scale of the universal Church. For while the Church may, through its canons, deter a presbyter from fulfilling his ministry outside his diocese of ordination, or its equivalent for religious, this is simply a matter of the good order of the community, not a reflection of the limitation of the presbyterate to a merely local ministry. *That* it is no longer. Every presbyter is ordained into the single presbyterium of the world-wide Church, though for the service of a particular church within it.

What, then, is a presbyter ordained for? He is ordained, first, to sanctify as priest: that is, to celebrate the sacraments. He is ordained, secondly, to teach as prophet: that is, to proclaim the Word and to instruct others in sound doctrine. He is ordained, thirdly, to govern as a shepherd: to put into effect the godly discipline which should mark the Church as a harmonious unity of persons living in public fidelity to God's declared will and way. But these three offices he carries out in dependence on the episcopate, since the episcopate (and not the presbyterate) is the fundamental continuing apostolic ministry in the Church.

All this will become clearer as the history of the sacrament of Order unfolds. But meanwhile, before leaving the ante-Nicene age, there is one last thing to note, since it is big with consequence for the future. As the early liturgical sources present ordination, the sacramental laying on of hands so consecrates the bishop and presbyter that they are, at a level which only the Holy Spirit can reach, suitably transformed. A new bond with the Son and Spirit is forged, so that the candidate is empowered to act by their strength in that ministry to which his ordination deputes him. We have here the seeds of the doctrine of the priestly 'character', a doctrine which will play a major part in the theology of Order in centuries to come. Though this doctrine is sometimes regarded as peculiarly Western, numerous texts from the Greek patristic tradition support it.[22] So does the early Church's practice: the refusal to re-ordain one who has been deposed and subsequently re-instated.[23]

The post-Nicene Church

If we turn now to the post-Nicene Church, we find that the assimilation of the new apostolic powers of the episcopate had led to fresh changes in the interrelation of bishop, presbyter and deacon at the local level. First of all: just as the apostles had a universal or ecumenical mandate, whilst they were also related to particular local churches which they had founded, so too the bishop ceased to be confined in his ministry to his own local church, even though he was a bishop only by reference to that church. Like the apostolic delegates, he became more concerned with the Church on a regional or universal basis, something most clearly attested in his role at councils. At councils, bishops took corporate decisions about particular local situations, in conscious continuity with the model of the apostolic council of Jerusalem in Acts 15. Such responsibilities, as well as the growth of the local church itself,[24] forced the bishop to devolve more of his local authority on to the presbyters. And so there emerges the 'parish priest': a presbyter who is the liturgist, teacher and pastor of a detached congregation occasionally visited by the bishop.

In one sense, this was a return to the more or less undifferentiated presbyter-bishops of the early Pauline communities, as in the Ephesus church in Acts 20. The new 'parish priest' (the term is of course anachronistic) is a combination, on a tiny scale, of the presbyter and the bishop of Hippolytus' *Apostolic Tradition*. But in those earlier communities, there had been a presbyteral council, modelled on the Seven. Here there is only one presbyter, a mini-version of the primitive bishop of Ignatius' *Letters*. By the fifth century, a hundred years or so after Nicaea, bishops in the East had even devolved to individual presbyters the right to confirm, to induct new laics, while retaining for themselves the right to consecrate the Confirmation oils, thus preserving, if in a less obvious form, the idea that it is the bishop, the head of the local church, who initiates new Christians into the 'order' of the laity. The same process of delegating Confirmation also got under way in the West. But there it was resisted by the — usually conservative — Roman church, under Pope Innocent I.

An unexpected result of this transferral of so many of the bishop's tasks as liturgist to the presbyterate was the emergence of the theory — not finally scotched until the Second Vatican Council — that there is no essential difference between the ministries of bishop and presbyter. On this view, the essential ministry in the Church is the presbyterate, and it is the presbyterate which has inherited the apostolic ministry, the episcopate being simply an ecclesiastical provision for securing good order among fellow-presbyters. As Jerome of Bethlehem (c.342-420) put it in the early fifth century:

48

What does a bishop do that a presbyter cannot, except ordain?[25]

Such views were fairly common in the post-Nicene period: Jerome's question receives its expected answer in John Chrysostom's (c.347–407) homilies on 1 Timothy:

> (Bishops) are superior to (presbyters) only in the power of ordination and in this respect alone have they advantage over presbyters.[26]

It seems likely that the starting-point of this idea lay in conflict between presbyters and deacons. Deacons could maintain that they were equal to, or even superior to, presbyters on the grounds of their special relationship with the bishop.[27] Presbyters responded by claiming parity with the bishops. They argued, as one would expect, from the example of the presbyter-bishops of the New Testament, just as sixteenth-century Presbyterians would do. This background of diaconal-presbyteral rivalry, with its warning of the dangers attached to ecclesiological ambiguity, is clearly expressed in the *Liber Quaestionum Veteris et Novi Testamenti,* a fourth-century work transmitted together with the writings of Augustine, but now ascribed to the unknown figure dubbed by the Renaissance 'Ambrosiaster'.[28] The claims of presbyters were powerfully assisted, not only by the increasing frequency with which they offered the Eucharist, not least for the dead, and on the anniversaries of the (heavenly) 'birthdays', *natalitia,* of the martyrs, but also by the delegation to them of the solemn or public, as distinct from clinical, celebration of baptism.[29] However, while a Church Father such as Chrysostom was willing to argue, in his comments on the address of Paul's Letter to Philippi, that, in the New Testament period, bishops and presbyters were the same people, the sole figure in the patristic age to assert the *absolute* identity of the two orders in the *contemporary* Church was Aërius of Pontus (fl.c.355), who received short shrift from that ever-vigilant guardian of orthodoxy, Epiphanius of Salamis (c.315–403), in his compendium of heretical opinions, the *Panarion.*[30] Yet a *tendency* of a 'presbyterianising' kind was relatively widespread, in both East and West. We shall see later that in the modern period, and most authoritatively in the documents of the Second Vatican Council, theologians proved able to disengage the element of truth in the (in itself, misconceived) notion of the (quasi-) parity of bishop and presbyter. The apostolic ministry does not pass through the presbyter, yet the presbyter receives, via the bishop, a share in that ministry none the less.

The emergence of the idea of the fundamental parity of episcopate and presbyterate was helped by the new tendency to call the presbyer a 'priest', *hiereus* in Greek, or, in Latin, *sacerdos,* a title originally reserved, as we have seen with Cyprian, to the bishop. In point of etymological fact, the English word 'priest' comes from an Anglo-Saxon contraction of 'presbyter', but the connotations which it developed in the course of the medieval centuries makes it more suitably a translation of *hiereus, sacerdos,* than of *presbyteros, presbyter.* The earliest evidence for calling presbyters 'priests' comes from memorials to deceased presbyters of the Asia Minor churches around 360, but it spread with remarkable rapidity in both East and West. The Pseudo-Ignatius (who expanded the corpus of Ignatian Letters) among the Greeks, Jerome and Ambrosiaster among the Latins, all regard it as perfectly normal usage in the late fourth-century Church.[31] This was, of course, a natural consequence of the presbyter becoming the normal celebrant of the Eucharist, itself the principal manifestation of the priestly office of the ordained ministry.

The logical outcome of this process is found in the churches of Ireland and Scotland, where bishops — according, at least, to one historiographical school — were retained simply in order to provide holy Orders for others, and lived otherwise secluded lives as monks in their monasteries, under the authority of abbots who themselves were simply presbyters.[32] Such abbots, in presbyteral orders, were the actual liturgists, teachers and pastors of the villages of a rural local church. Irish-Scottish missionaries in Europe after the fall of the Western Roman

Empire took such practices, and their accompanying notions, overseas: when the Irish monk Virgilius became Bishop of Salzburg in 745 he governed his church from the monastery of St Peter whose abbot he was. Remaining a presbyter for a further twenty years, he simply made use of the bishop's Orders of one of his own monks, a certain Dub-dá-Crich.[33] By and large, however, the rest of the Western Church did not follow the Celtic practice. It retained sufficient grip on its primitive tradition to see to it that bishops retained what became known as 'jurisdiction', namely, that pastoral authority which is exercised in the Church in the name of the apostles themselves.[34]

Now that we have a better understanding of the development of the ordained ministries we can see that the similarity of function of bishop and presbyter in the period after Nicaea is not a survival of pre-Nicene practice but something new. Pre-Nicene texts like the *Apostolic Tradition,* itself discovered within the last century, show that, before Nicaea, the offices of bishop and presbyter were as different as those of bishop and deacon.[35] What has happened is — to summarise what we have just seen — that the apostolic ministry, incorporated into the local ministry in the office of the bishop, affected the rest of the local ministry, and especially the presbyterate, by forcing the bishop to delegate some episcopal functions in the local church so as to have more time and energy for his wider responsibilities.

Just as in the post-Nicene Church the bishop's presbyteral college split up and became individual parish priests, so also the *deacons* were increasingly separated from the bishop. They became scattered over a diocese, which was no longer a city but an entire civil province, and attached to presbyters as their assistants. Rarely in the future would a deacon play so great a part in a Church crisis as Athanasius (c.296-373) played as his bishop's adviser at Nicaea; though, even as late as the eleventh century, the Roman archdeacon was a power to reckon with. As usual the Roman church preserved an older structure, and kept the close link between deacon and bishop.

51

Another factor in the comparative decline of the diaconate was the late fourth-century idea of Orders as a series of graded steps: a *cursus honorum*.[36] To reach one you must pass through the one before it; you cannot take leaps for example, from layman to bishop. On this view, Orders are related to each other like a series of Chinese boxes, each higher order containing the powers of that below it. Thus, whereas Cyprian was ordained by jumping — *per saltum* — from layman to the episcopate, Ambrose (c.339-397), a hundred years later, was elected bishop of Milan while still a catechumen (something even more startling by modern standards) received baptism, confirmation, minor orders, the diaconate, and the presbyterate on successive days before receiving the episcopate. Both systems, the *per saltum* method, and the *cursus honorum,* remain, so far as Church teaching is concerned, equal possibilities. A case can be made out for each of the two. The older system, ordination *per saltum,* highlights the relation of each ministry to the needs of the local church at a given time. It also sees the ministries as part of an organic whole. Further, it reduces the danger of ecclesiastical careerism. The newer system, ordination in a *cursus honorum,* ensures that no one will inherit the full apostolic ministry — that is, become a bishop — who has not served the Church as a deacon and carried the everyday burden of the ministry of the Word and sacraments as a presbyter.

This is, perhaps, a convenient point to note that the words *ordo* and *ordinatio,* like many of their fellows in the Roman liturgical books, have a civil origin, transformed by specifically Christian usage. *Ordinatio* was the term used at Rome for appointing civil functionaries to their office: Jerome uses it as a synonym for the Greek *cheirotonia,* the laying on of hands, in his commentary on the Book of Isaiah.[37] Those so inducted into office, or otherwise distinguished from the general body of the populace, were, in ancient Rome, an *ordo* — which thus became, at Christian hands, the proper term for the clergy's special place within the people of God.[38]

Worth noting from this period, and mentioned above in

connection with Ambrose, is the appearance of the so-called minor orders.[39] These offices arrived on the scene in the fourth century as variegated forms of assistance to the deacon. Their number fluctuated. In the East there were often only two — sub-deacon and lector; in the West there were generally five: sub-deacon, acolyte, exorcist, lector and porter. Already practised in the sixth-century Roman church was a rite of admitting new candidates to this entire series of offices. A prayer 'for the making of clerics' was offered over them, and they were tonsured, as an outer sign of their new condition.[40] Minus the tonsure, the ceremony survives in the Latin rite of the period after the Second Vatican Council under the (fairly obvious) title of 'candidacy'.

Other titles which occur were cantor, translator, keeper of the graveyard, and one female category which we shall be looking at later — deaconess. The explosion of minor orders in the patristic Church was, in fact, comparable with the explosion of ministries in the Roman Catholicism of the last decade. Numerically, it could be on a vast scale: the Church of the Holy Wisdom at Constantinople, in the time of Justinian in the sixth century, had on its staff, apart from sixty priests and one hundred deacons, forty deaconesses, ninety sub-deacons, one hundred and ten lectors, twenty-five cantors and one hundred doorkeepers. Presumably what fuelled this movement were such things as the desire for richness of total effect, for efficient organisation and, perhaps, the wish to give as many people as possible a part, however modest, to play. We shall be looking later at the degree to which such ministerial explosions are a good thing.

Many of these characters were, like their modern counterparts, non-ordained, in the sense that there was no laying-on of hands — the crucial sacramental gesture found at all times in the tradition. However, there are two caveats to be entered here. First, in some parts of the Church a distinction arose between two kinds of laying-on of hands, one performed *at* the altar, *cheirotonia,* and the other performed *away* from it, *cheirothesia,* the second being made more freely available to ministers in grades other than those of the classical threefold ministry, and notably to sub-deacons, lectors and deaconesses. Secondly, and perhaps connected with this, as time went on, the ordination ceremony of bishop, presbyter and deacon grew richer in its symbolism and so, inevitably more complicated. As a result, theologians, especially in the medieval period, would come to lose sight of the centrality of the laying on of hands as the 'matter' of Order, its central sacramental sign. Once the idea had been floated that the crucial sacramental gesture in ordination to the presbyterate might be the 'handing over of the instruments', *porrectio instrumentorum,* that is, giving the candidate the sacred vessels, the chalice and the paten — then it became possible to think of the sub-diaconate as an order in the full sense, a major order, because the sub-deacon received an empty chalice on his institution, as a symbol of his duty to assist the deacon at the Liturgy. Even as late as the Council of Trent there was doubt in many people's minds as to whether the sub-diaconate might not be a genuine part of the Church's sacramental ordering, a differentiation of the apostolic ministry, rather than simply an ecclesiastical creation. This is why Trent (DS 1776) describes the threefold ministry as bishops, presbyters and *ministers,* following its usual principle not to define as doctrine something which was still regarded as unsettled by the majority of theologians.

So much for the organisation of the ministry in the early Church. It is time now to turn to the actual theology written about the ordained ministry by the Fathers. It may be said at once that the only systematic reflection on the sacrament of Order which has come down to us from the classic period of the patristic Church — if we except the contribution of the Pseudo-Denys,[41] who belonged to the Monophysite, or, at any rate, Monophysite-tending, penumbra of Eastern Catholicism — is that of Augustine of Hippo (354-430). Other patristic treatises look hopeful when judged by reference to their titles. But, on inspection, they turn out to be works of what might now be termed the spirituality of the priesthood — the moral and religious qualities required of a bishop or priest

— which is not to say that they contain no nuggets of doctrinal insight here and there. I have in mind such writings as Gregory Nazianzen's (329-389) *Second Oration,* sometimes called the *Apologia de fuga sua,* the 'explanation of his flight', since it describes how he vainly tried to evade ordination to the presbyterate; Ambrose of Milan's *On the Duties,* sometimes called *On the Duties of the Ministers;* John Chrysostom's *On the Priesthood* and Pope Gregory the Great's (c.540-604) *Pastoral Rule,* called in England from Anglo-Saxon times, *Pastoral Care.* I will return to these texts in a moment. Meanwhile, let us turn to the dogmatically meatier diet provided by Augustine.

Augustine's treatment of Order is found principally in his writings about the schism of the Donatists, the *pars donatista,* a 'part' which, in all probability, formed the majority of North African Christians during Augustine's lifetime. The origins of the Donatist schism are controverted, and indeed were at the time. Suffice it to say that, according to the Donatists, the holiness of the episcopate is a necessary condition for the apostolic continuity of the Church. Hence, if the Catholic Church has within its episcopate men who are reconciled *traditores,* that is, individuals who, under persecution, handed over the Church's Scriptures as a token of their apostasy, then it no longer has the apostolic ministry and so is no longer the apostolic Church. The apostolic ministry and Church endure only with those bishops and people who withdraw from the Catholic Church to form the Donatist *pars,* or portion. One of the problems which faced Augustine in bringing the Donatist schism to an end concerned an obvious question which helped to concentrate the mind on what the sacrament of Order is for, and what the conditions are on which it is held.

Were those bishops consecrated by the seceding group of Catholic bishops *true* bishops — albeit schismatic bishops — and was the sacramental life they had brought about in their own schismatic communities a *genuine* sacramental life? Hitherto, the presumption in North African Catholicism, nowhere clearer than in Cyprian, had been that there are, in fact, no sacraments outside the visible Church — that is, outside the visibly united Church. The reasoning behind this belief was quite forceful, and remains the dominant theology of sacramental genuineness in Eastern Orthodoxy to this day. The ministry of the Word and sacraments depends for its authenticity, so it was argued, on the apostolic commission enjoyed by the Church. If a particular community or group of communities breaks away from the communion of the single apostolic Church, then it cannot take an authentic ministry of Word and sacraments with it. And this is so even if it happens to preserve a tactile succession of episcopal leaders.

However, the practice of the wider Church before Augustine was by no means as clear-cut as this theory would suggest. Not all schism was regarded as being *from* the Church. People also admitted the possibility of schism *within* the Church — most famously, in the case of a schism at Antioch in the fourth century when great sees and Fathers were found supporting different sides. Such schisms were generally started off by disagreements over Church practice leading to jurisdictional disputes between rival claimants to sees, though some, such as that between Rome and many Eastern sees over the orthodoxy of the Antiochene doctors in the later fifth century, had wider implications. No one proposed that schisms of this kind destroyed the sacramental reality of the apostolic ministry for either of the parties involved.

Augustine offered an answer to the question of how there can be a genuine ordained ministry, and so a true proclamation of the Word and celebration of the sacraments, in schismatic communities whose leaders were themselves ordained according to the Church's normal practice. Augustine's solution, which became virtually universal in the Western half of the Church, was to distinguish between validity and liceity. Illicitly celebrated sacraments might still be valid sacraments: a distinction never previously made in this way. Some commentators point out that, taken to its logical conclusion, the Augustinian concept of validity of Order could produce fairly unsatisfactory results. For it entailed that in principle it was possible, owing to a series of historical contingencies, to have valid Orders outside the Church's unity, combined with heretical views on most subjects, including the sacrament of Order itself, while, conversely, by a different set of historical contingencies, there might be invalid Orders within some parts of the Church — owing to accidental rupture in the tactile succession — despite the complete orthodoxy, ecclesial obedience and good faith of those concerned.

What Augustine might have made of such so-called logical consequences of his concept of the validity of Orders we do not know, whereas we do know that he made one major concession to the older Cyprianic view which had considered Church and Order together and not as separable realities. Augustine made this major concession by drawing a *second* important distinction in his theology of Order: a distinction, this time between validity and *fruitfulness*. Not all valid sacraments are fruitful sacraments, in the full sense of that phrase. In other words, the fact of schism, the objectively sinful context of celebrating validly but illicitly a schismatic sacrament, partly suspends the grace of that sacrament, without, however, nullifying it altogether. Granted that the grace of the sacraments must be related to the purpose of the sacraments — namely, to manifest and increase our unity with God and so with each other, the schismatic celebration of the sacraments cannot leave that grace unaffected. Sacramental grace will only be fully released on the reconciliation of those concerned with the single, visibly united Church. Let us hear Augustine in his own words: noting that, for him, the heart of the matter is baptism — the key sacrament of salvation, the gateway to ecclesial living, so that ordination becomes, above all, the sacrament which enables the Church's ministers to confer baptism, itself including, in his day, confirmation. In the opening chapter of *On Baptism,* Augustine points out that:

> those who in the sacrilege of schism depart from the communion of the Church, certainly retain the grace of baptism, which they received before their departure, seeing that, in case of their return, it is not again conferred

on them; whence it is proved, that what they had received while within the unity of the Church, they could not have lost in their separation. But if it can be retained outside, why may it not also be given there? If you say, 'It is not rightly given without the pale;' we answer, 'As it is not rightly retained, and yet is in some sense retained, so it is not indeed rightly given, but yet it is given'. But as, by reconciliation to unity, that begins to be profitably possessed which was possessed to no profit in exclusion from unity, so, by the same reconciliation, that begins to be profitable which without it was given to no profit.

Drawing out the relevance of these principles for ordination, Augustine goes on:

> ... the sacrament of baptism is what the person possesses who is baptised; and the sacrament of conferring baptism is what he possesses who is ordained. And as the baptised person, if he depart from the unity of the Church, does not thereby lose the sacrament of baptism, so also he who is ordained, if he depart from the unity of the Church, does not lose the sacrament of conferring baptism.[42]

And he defends the Catholic practice of the time by saying:

> We act rightly who do not dare to repudiate God's sacraments, even when administered in schism.[43]

Augustine accepts, then, the validity of schismatic ordinations, but denies full spiritual fruitfulness to the sacraments which schismatic ministers themselves celebrate.

Augustine does not simply argue that the Catholic practice of treating schismatic baptisms and ordinations as valid yet lacking in full spiritual fruitfulness is consistent. He also shows that it is intelligible by analysis of what the situation of schism entails. As he explains, it includes both positive and negative elements.

> If...a man who has severed himself from unity wishes to do anything different from that which had been impressed

on him while in the state of unity, in this point he does sever himself, and is no longer a part of the united whole; but wherever he desires to conduct himself as is customary in the state of unity, in which he himself learned and received the lessons which he seeks to follow, in these points he remains a member, and is united to the corporate whole.[44]

So far as the issue of schismatic ordinations is concerned, we might wish to let the views of Cyprian and Augustine modify each other, allowing that communities whose communion with the Catholic Church has been ruptured — such as the Eastern Orthodox or the Old Catholics — do indeed retain the apostolic succession, and so the fullness of the ordained ministry, but denying that this process is indefinitely extensible. In particular, an individual member of the episcopate, should he break communion with the Church and attempt to set up an *ecclesiola,* a 'mini-church' of his own, cannot necessarily be regarded as creating validly ordained ministers of the Word and sacraments with apostolic disciplinary authority, even though he himself was duly initiated into the apostolic ministry. Such an attempt to balance the Augustinian and Cyprianic views seems necessary to deal sensibly with such characters as *episcopi vagantes,* 'wandering bishops', often without either *presbyteria* or laity.[45] This is an issue to which the medievals also gave some thought, as we will be seeing later.

Finally, Augustine also tries to convince the Donatists not only that the practice of the Catholic Church in these matters is consistent and intelligible, but that their own view that any grave personal sins of a minister invalidate the sacraments he confers implies a misunderstanding of the nature of ordination itself. For ordination makes one precisely a minister — that is, a servant or instrument of Christ, the Head of the Church. The efficacy of the Church's sacraments derives wholly from Christ, and not in any way from the ordained themselves. In celebrating the rites of the Church they become vehicles of Christ, and as such, their moral excellence or lack of it does not enter into the reckoning. And in any case, given that a morally blameless reputation on the part of an ordained man might just be the result of skill in hypocrisy or deceit, there could be no certainty of the grace bestowed through the sacraments were the Donatists correct. It is worth noting in this connection that Augustine held schism to be, essentially, a moral failing rather than, like heresy, a crime against faith. He saw schism as, basically, an offence against fraternal charity. The sacraments administered by an ordained minister who is morally unworthy, through the moral collapse which is schism, of celebrating them, are unaffected by his personal guilt. They are not 'his' sacraments, but those of God and the Church. This conviction that the ordained, in performing their priestly office, are simply instruments of Christ the Head, acting in his *persona,* playing his part so that he may act through their instrumentality, would become a permanent acquisition of Catholic teaching. The ordained are 'signed', 'stamped', 'sealed', with that particular christological 'character'.[46]

A full account of Augustine's presentation of the ordained ministry would have to take into account also his many exhortations to his own clergy, together with his own practice as what the Dutch patristic scholar Frederick van der Meer called, in his evocative yet detailed study of Augustine the bishop, a 'pastor of souls'.[47] This reminder may serve to link the largely dogmatic account of Augustine's teaching offered here to the four patristic treatises on the moral and spiritual qualities of the ordained, which have come down to us from the pens of Gregory Nazianzen, Ambrose, John Chrysostom and Gregory the Great.

Gregory Nazianzen's contribution is his second *Oration,* an explanation of his angry departure from his father's congregation after the said father, a local bishop, pressed him, none too gently, into accepting ordination. To this, Gregory added an account of the duties of the ordained ministry. Gregory speaks of the ministry in terms of the 'pastors and teachers' of Paul's Letter to the Ephesians. He understands the role of a priest or bishop as one of guiding others to perfection, both by helping them to understand what this requires, as a teacher, and in assisting them to realise such teaching in practice, as a pastor. His main metaphor for both sorts of activity is medical: the priest is a 'physician of souls'. As he writes:

> ... the guiding of man, that most variable and manifold of creatures, seems to me in very deed to be the art of arts and science of sciences. Any one may recognise this, by comparing the work of the physician of souls with the treatment of the body; and noticing that, laborious as the latter is, ours is more laborious, and of more consequence, from the nature of its subject-matter, the power of its science, and the object of its exercise.[48]

En passant, Gregory mentions aspects of the priest's role other than this therapeutic one. Thus, he speaks of the presbyter or bishop as a liturgist, one called to celebrate 'those mystic and elevating rites which are our greatest and most precious privilege.' And he touches on an aspect of the pastoral office dear to Paul in his dealings with the Church at Corinth: the importance of 'order and rule', as opposed to 'anarchy and disorder' in the Church. Finally, Gregory takes it for granted that the ordained should excel in what he calls 'virtue and nearness to God'. It was precisely because he considered that he personally did not so excel that he had tried to evade ordination.

This stress on the spiritual and ethical standard which the ordained man should set the laity is picked up by Ambrose in his book *On the Duties,* later called *On the Duties of Ministers,* because it originated in a series of talks given by Ambrose to the junior clergy of the church of Milan shortly after he became their bishop in 373. In this treatise, Ambrose casts himself in the role of the 'teacher', *didaskalos,* of Ephesians, though by his own account he does this partly out of humility, since it is the last (and therefore presumably the least) ministry mentioned by Paul in that letter.[49] Ambrose had been civil governor of Milan before his election as bishop, and he drew on his own formation as an administrator in the Roman imperial system to structure these addresses. More specifically, just as the Roman politician-philosopher Cicero had written a treatise *On Duties* for his son, a document meant to pass on the sense of the highest ethical ideals of Roman public life, so now Ambrose, who was aware of his own lack of biblical and theological education, will do something similar for his own clergy. It is difficult to know what weight to attach to Ambrose's claim for the bishop of the office of a *didaskalos,* but his example contributed to the tradition of theologian-bishop left behind by the patristic Church and to some degree under reconstruction today. Probably, Ambrose's conferences were not written up until around 388, by which time he had acquired a great deal of exegetical and theological erudition. But he never seems to have quite decided whether he wanted to publish a general treatise on the nature of Christian ethics, or a work for the clergy in particular. This did not prevent his treatise being very influential, in the sense that, in the later patristic and early medieval periods, a whole chain of handbooks on the duties of the ordained have come down to us, inspired to a greater or lesser degree by his work, but placing their emphasis increasingly on the liturgical duties of those in Orders, something which is simply taken for granted in Ambrose — as we can infer from his references to the familiarity of his hearers with the liturgical use of the Bible.

Let us move on to the third of these patristic exhortations to the ordained: John Chrysostom's *On the Priesthood.* As historical accident has it, it was written at approximately the same time as Ambrose's treatise, around 388, and describes events from the year when Ambrose's material was first given an airing in oral form, namely, 374. The events in question — pressurisation into priesthood — were reminiscent both of Gregory Nazianzen's ordination as a presbyter, and Ambrose's consecration as a bishop; the difference was that John Chrysostom was actually successful (at the time) in evading ordination, which he avoided by taking to the mountains near his native Antioch to lead a contemplative — basically an eremitic — life. Like Gregory, by whose second *Oration* he was surely influenced, Chrysostom sees the priest's task (whether as presbyter or bishop) in primarily pastoral terms. He has a very exalted view of the pastoral office. Referring to the encounter between penitent Peter and the risen Christ at the end of St John's Gospel, Chrysostom points out that Christ might have said to Peter:

> If you love me: practice fasting, sleep on the ground, prolong your vigils, defend the oppressed, be a father to the orphans, a husband to the widow that bore them. But passing over all these things, what does he say? 'Shepherd my sheep'.[50]

The benefit of the pastoral office, writes Chrysostom, 'extends to the whole people'.

> He who distributes alms to the needy or otherwise defends the oppressed benefits his neighbour to some extent; but these corporal benefits are as much less than the spiritual benefits conferred by the priest as the body is inferior to the soul.[51]

Chrysostom devotes much more attention than Gregory Nazianzen and Ambrose to the liturgical functions of a priest. Because of the holiness of the Eucharist which he celebrates, the New Testament ministerial priest exercises a more august office than his Old Testament predecessors. For in the Eucharist as sacrifice the Lord himself lies immolated on the altar, while in his prayer for the people, the priest calls down not fire from heaven, as with Elijah of old, but the Holy Spirit himself. These two points are made by way of argument for Chrysostom's claim that:

> Though the office of the priesthood is exercised on earth, it ranks nevertheless, in the order of celestial things — and rightly so. It was neither man nor an angel nor an archangel nor any other created power, but the Paraclete himself who established this ministry, and who ordained that men abiding in the flesh should imitate the ministry

of the angels. For that reason, it behoves the bearer of the priesthood to be as pure as if he stood in the very heavens amidst those powers.[52]

Chrysostom's portrait of the good priest combines the high ascetic ideals of the monastic movement with a healthy dose of common sense. The priest should practise sobriety and vigilance, that is, asceticism, but even more important is a capacity to control one's temper, so necessary when dealing all day long with all sorts and conditions of people. Chrysostom also lays stress on the need for the priest to know his doctrine, and his theology. He must be prepared to meet the arguments of Jews, heretics or pagans, and be skilled in answering the questions of the faithful about their religion. Finally, the priest for Chrysostom is an intercessor. He draws near to God by interceding for all sinners, whether living or dead.

> as if the whole world were his responsibility, and he were the father of all men...[53]

Like Ezekiel whom he cites,[54] Chrysostom considers that the priest will be held to account for the spiritual death of his children; his sins will be punished more rigorously than those of the laity. These negative conclusions are based in part on a positive principle in Chrysostom's soteriology. As he writes:

> I do not believe it possible for a man to be saved who has done nothing to advance the salvation of his neighbour.[55]

Finally, we must look at a treatise which had a unique impact in England, namely the *Pastoral Rule* of Pope Gregory the Great. Written, according to some, as an attempt by Gregory to give the secular clergy a counterpart to the monastic *Regula Benedicti,* the 'Rule of Saint Benedict' (and other monastic rules known to him), the *Pastoral Rule* was, however, known in England as the *Pastoral Care,* a title drawn from its opening words. Given that, at the centre of Gregory's thought lay the *cura animarum,* the preparation of souls for the Second Coming, a priority for his public policy was the creation of a pastorally inclined clergy — and notably episcopate — trained in preaching and teaching.[56] Originating, like the works of Nazianzen and Chrysostom as an apology for the author's wish to escape the office of a bishop, it proved enormously influential. Translated into Greek in Gregory's lifetime by order of the Byzantine emperor Maurice, it was brought to England by Gregory's envoy, the missionary monk Augustine. In the ninth century King Alfred translated it into West Saxon with the aid of some of his clergy, and arranged for every bishop to have a copy. In the empire of Charlemagne, it was given to each new bishop at his consecration. The Anglican biographer of Gregory wrote of it:

> The ideal which Gregory upheld was for centuries the ideal of the clergy of the West, and through them the spirit of the great Pope governed the Church, long after his body had been laid to rest beneath the pavement of St Peter's.[57]

In fact, most of Gregory's book is devoted to questions of how to deal pastorally with various kinds of individual or group, and, in particular, how to preach to them effectively, especially where the moral life is concerned. A librarian could quite reasonably classify it as a treatise on the art of preaching. One interesting wider concern in the *Pastoral Rule,* however, is how the pastor should unite the contemplative and active lives in his ministry. As Gregory puts it,

> He must not be remiss in his care for the inner life by preoccupation with the external, nor must he in his solicitude for what is internal, fail to give attention to the external.[58]

What the age of the Fathers will pass on to its successors — and not least to the drafters of the decree of the Second Vatican Council on the priesthood is, then, a sense for the *constellation of tasks* that defines the work of the ordained. Both in the ordination prayers of the patristic Church, and in the

65

theological comments of individual Fathers, the *pattern* of the ordained life, not least in its presbyteral form, is becoming clear.

3

The Medieval Theology of Order

The early Middle Ages

The theology of Order in the Western church between Augustine and the early twelfth-century beginnings of Christian Scholasticism was a somewhat restricted affair. In this area, as in others, Western theology was indebted first and foremost to Augustine (that is, after the Bible). It centred on the fundamental problem which Augustine had left his successors in his anti-Donatist references to Order. The nature of the problem may be expressed in terms of a tension between two 'sub-traditions' in the Church. One of these, the Augustinian, affirmed that there could be true sacraments, including Order, outside the Church's unity; the other, the Cyprianic, denied this.[1] As we saw in the last chapter, there may be some ecclesial situations where we find ourselves warranted in calling in the Cyprianic tradition as a counterpoise to what seem the unacceptable logical consequences of Augustine's position. In theology, as elsewhere, it is crucial to intellectual judgment to know just how far any given principle should be pressed, and when some other principle should be invoked to redress a balance thought worthy of preserving. The issue of genuineness of Orders called for especially nice evaluation, since it could so easily produce an *imbroglio* of practical complications.

The coming of Christianity to Anglo-Saxon England furnishes an example. The Byzantine church tended to reject ordination by heretics. When, therefore, the Cilician monk Theodore became Archbishop of Canterbury, he set aside the ordinations carried out by the Northumbrian Ceadda of Lichfield, on the grounds that two British bishops, whom Theodore regarded as 'Quartodeciman' heretics for their faulty calculation of Easter, had served as Ceadda's co-consecrators at York.[2] Theodore's penitentiary[3] insisted on the outright or 'absolute' (re-)ordination of heretics,[4] and the waters of the Roman church's own practice were muddied by the decision of a synod in 769 to declare null the ordinations of the anti-pope Constantine, on no other grounds than those of his usurpation of the papal office.[5] A learned cleric of the Carolingian era looking back on the tangle of conflicting precedents and texts, could only suppose that the Church used, in alternating fashion, both rigour and indulgence, and thus make sense of his authorities by appeal to the 'power of dispensation' which she enjoyed.[6]

In the course of time, the underlying conflict of Cyprianic and Augustinian sub-traditions came to the surface in explicit statements of the opposing rationales. Peter Damian's (1007-1072) *Liber gratissimus* is frankly Augustinian: schism and simony are evils, but their malice cannot obstruct God's grace since

> that living spring is in no way damned up, but to the end of the Age flows through the forest of the Church, so that, not only the sacerdotal order but all those reborn in Christ may draw from it the draught of their salvation.[7]

Humbert of Silva Candida (d.1061), by contrast, is uncompromisingly Cyprianic: the sacraments of schismatics, heretics, simoniacs, are null and void.[8]

Yet, between the two theories, an intermediate position of some kind found, in the words of the historian of this tangled subject, 'illustrious patrons'.[9] A German theologian, Bernold of Constance (c.1054-1100), was perhaps the first eleventh century mind to seek to mediate between the two traditions. He argued that only the sacraments of those schismatic ministers who were originally ordained as Catholics continue to be valid beyond the Church's unity.[10] Sacraments administered by those ordained at the hands of such lapsed bishops (and presbyters) cannot be relied on. In effect, Bernold suggested that the Augustinian principle operates for just one sacramental generation, after which the Cyprianic principle takes over. Though men take the Church's sacraments with them into schism, they have no apostolic mandate to reproduce a sacramental ministry in others. Later, however, as a result of wider reading and notably of Augustine's *De baptismo,* Bernold preferred to regard sacraments administered in long-standing schismatic communities as genuine, yet ineffective to salvation. In this, he was much impressed by the practice of such patristic popes as Leo I and Gregory the Great. To these he counterposed, unflatteringly, later Roman synods which had set aside, in a period of both ecclesiastical and theological confusion, simoniac and schismatic Orders. They took place, he wrote reprovingly, at a time when 'much that was against right and law was usurpingly perpetrated'.[11] Despite these strictures, and Bernold's own re-thinking, his earlier ideas on the subject maintained themselves in such slightly later figures as Bruno of Segni, the theological adviser of Pope Urban II.[12]

Again, the Flemish theologian Alger of Liège (d.1131/2) posed the problem as to whether a misunderstanding of the Gospel, on the part of some schismatic group, could be so radical as to abrogate the 'normal' functioning of the Augustinian principle. He suggested that the Church could recognise, for instance, Arian sacraments, but not, say, those of Unitarians — of sects which denied the doctrine of the Trinity in *any* form.[13] Since the Creed is Trinitarian in structure, such sects could be said to have departed from the faith of the Church in an absolute way which justified invoking the Cyprianic principle, and denying that they possess a genuine sacrament life — a life where the Christian mystery is supremely expressed in visible signs instituted by the Son and filled with holiness by the Spirit, and so a life based on faith in the Trinity.

The drawbacks of an unconditional adherence to the Augustinian principle are well illustrated by the ideas of the twelfth-century theologian Gandulph of Bologna (fl.1160-70). He summed up his theology of the ordained ministry in the motto, *Ordo est ambulatorius,* which may be translated, 'Order keeps on walking'. For Gandulph, Order is indefinitely extensible outside the bounds of the visible Church, irrespective of the intention of the one who is ordaining, or of the one receiving ordination. Here Gandulph was misled into exaggerating the sheer objectivity of the sacramental Order, which he treated as wholly separable from the mind of the Church.[14]

An interesting attempt to apply to Order Augustine's concept of how the grace of schismatic baptism exists in a latent or suppressed form in those baptised outside the Church was made by another Bolognese doctor, Master Rufinus (d.c.1192). Rufinus suggested that a schismatic bishop has only a *potestas aptitudinis,* a 'power that is apt for' episcopal ministry. In actuality — in practice — this capacity is null. The 'aptitude' can only be released when the schismatic minister is reconciled to the Church.[15]

A fuller picture of how the pre-Scholastic Middle Ages saw the sacrament of Order would involve the consultation of a huge variety of texts: ordination rites, homilies and commentaries on passages of Scripture relevant to episcopate, presbyterate, diaconate; *capitularia,* with their disciplinary instructions for the exercise of these offices; manuals for the education of the clergy; treatises on ecclesiastical vestments, and that tradition, already mentioned, of composing works on the liturgical duties of ordained ministers with titles based on Ambrose's *De officiis.*[16] From this medley of sources, two themes in particular may be singled out.

First, there is an emerging concern that the whole way of life of the ordained person will be consonant with the sacred functions which he accepts at his ordination. For example: treatises on the significance of ecclesiastical vestments, of which the anonymous Germanic *De vestimentis sacerdotalibus* may be the parent, find in those vestments signs of the *virtues* which their wearers should practise.[17] The anointing of a presbyter's hands during the ordination ritual itself, a practice probably originating in the Celtic churches, symbolised not only the power of Eucharistic consecration but also, or alternatively, the purification of the candidate. Thus in Amalarius of Metz' (c.780-850/1) *Liber officialis,* the ordinand's hands are anointed:

> that they may be clean to offer sacrifices to God and be generous in performing the other works of mercy...

and Amalarius adds that

> both the grace of healing and the charity of love are signified by the oil.[18]

Another Carolingian divine, Theodulph of Orléans, focused his interpretation exclusively on the holiness of life which the presbyter needs if he is to be an example to the flock.[19] (Both topics, vestments and the anointing, were approached by way of a spiritual interpretation, 'typological' or allegorical, of the Old Testament characters, Aaron and his sons, the founders of the Jewish priesthood in biblical perspective.) The high point of this growing ethical concern, within the medieval period, is the allocution added by William Durandus (1230/1-1296), the author of the most comprehensive and influential of the treatises *De officiis,* to the bishop's book for use in ordaining, the Pontifical. Although elements of this address, and notably its list of presbyteral functions, can be found in late patristic sources in the West, the portions newly added by Durandus are exhortations to holiness of life. And here the key words, still found in the contemporary Roman Pontifical today, are: '*Agnoscite quod agitis: imitamini quod tractatis:* 'acknowledge what it is you do: imitate that which you handle'. In other words:

> Durand wishes to make the celebration of the Eucharist a further motive for sanctity. The presbyters must strive to enact in their lives that which they touch and handle in the sacrament of the Eucharist, wherein is celebrated the mystery of the Lord's death. Here they have a motive for the mortification of their bodies, since as ministers of the sacrament they ought to copy in their lives the death of the Lord which they celebrate.[20]

This ethical and spiritual interest in the holy living of the ordained man will not, however, receive really sustained and systematic attention until after the close of the medieval period: in the Council of Trent and the Catholic reforming saints who strove to implement its decrees and its vision.

The second theme which might be extracted from the scattered pieces of the early medieval mosaic is the heightened awareness of the offering of the Eucharistic sacrifice as the priestly task *par excellence* — though by no means to the exclusion of the rest of the functions of the ordained. We have already noted how the formulae accompanying the rite of anointing make frequent mention of the consecration of the Eucharistic elements, and the offering of the Eucharistic sacrifice which that consecration entails. The popularity of the Old Testament type of the priesthood of Aaron encouraged emphasis on the cultic duties of presbyter and bishop, of which the Mass formed the chief. But the early medieval doctors were far from seeing the sacrament of Order as nothing other than a necessary means to the provision of the Eucharist. When discussing the etymology of the very word *sacerdos*, generally construed, on the authority of Isidore of Seville (c.560-636), as deriving from *sanctificando*, and hence from *sacrum dans*, these divines found in the latter phrase a portmanteau term with room for more than the Mass. Rabanus Maurus (776 or 784-856), for example, understands the 'giving of the holy' as the ordained minister's celebration of baptism, and his preaching of the Word, as well as his distributing the Body and Blood of the Lord in holy communion.[21] Honorius of Autun (early twelfth century) and Amalarius of Metz, following Bede, thought that *sacerdos* originally meant *sacer dux,* 'a holy leader': thus emphasising the pastoral office of the ordained even as they applied to presbyter and bishop a term with an otherwise primarily cultic resonance.[22] The Ordinals in use in the Latin church likewise listed a variety of tasks as the proper purview of the ordained, and these, in different forms, always show a continuing awareness of the threefold *munus,* priestly, prophetic and pastoral.[23] However, a touch more clarity and system was definitely a desideratum for the future.

The age of Scholasticism

The attempt to write a more lucid theology of Order, a feature of the new flowering of theological life in the dawn of Scholasticism, begins with the *On the Sacraments* of Hugh of St-Victor (c.1096-1141). For Hugh, Order can be known to be a sacrament by reference to its three exemplifying qualities at one and the same time. It is, first of all, something that the Church initiates by a liturgical action; secondly, it is something she understands as conveying not simply office, but, more than office, spiritual power; and thirdly, it is something which brings with it not only office-with-spiritual power but also the grace of Christ.[24]

Peter Lombard's (c.1100-1160) account of Order in book four of his *Sentences* gave, however, the fullest account of this sacrament before the period of High Scholasticism, the great masters.[25] Influenced by Hugh of St-Victor and the canonical sources marshalled by Gratian, Lombard's account would prove, thanks to the popularity of his textbook, the foundation on which the major Scholastics built their own theology of this sacrament. For Peter Lombard, Order is a sevenfold sacramental reality, each of whose offices has been fulfilled by Jesus Christ in 'typical' anticipation of the ministry of his Church. Just as the Lord himself chased out the money-lenders from the Jerusalem temple, so now Christian 'door-keepers' (the first of the minor orders) preside at the entrance to churches, mindful of their Saviour's words, 'I am the Gate' (Jn 10:9). The lectors, who have the task of singing the lessons and psalms of the Liturgy, can remember that Christ himself read and commented the holy books of Judaism. Exorcists, who are called to address and expel evil spirits in God's name, need not search far in the Gospels to find Jesus doing the very same thing. The 'acolytes', *ceroferarii,* who light and carry candles and torches in the Church's offices, do so in order to symbolise the joy entering the world through the one who proclaimed himself its light (Jn 8:12). The sub-deacons, who assist the deacons in the Mass, were prefigured when the Lord washed the feet of his own disciples, as recorded in the Gospel of John

(Jn 13:1-20). As for deacons themselves, Christ fulfilled their particular office in distributing to his apostles his own Body and Blood at the Last Supper, and when, in the Garden of the Agony, he called on his disciples to persevere in prayer (Lk 22:28). The seventh and final order in Lombard's catalogue is that of presbyters, who are not only *seniores* but also *sacerdotes,* though lacking the 'apex' of priesthood which belongs to the bishop alone. The differentiation of the presbyters and bishops reflects that of the Seventy and the Twelve in the years of Jesus' public ministry. What they share is the priestly office, which Christ exercised on the altar of the Cross, where he offered himself as both priest and victim, a sacrifice already made in principle in the Upper Room, with the conversion of bread and wine into his own Body and his life's Blood.

Lombard also recorded the views of his medieval predecessors on a range of disputed questions centring on the issues of schismatic and simoniac ordination. He suspended judgement on these issues, as well as on the by now classic *crux:* are presbyterate and episcopate the same order, that is, the same grade of Order, merely two degrees of dignity within it? Or, alternatively, are they really two *kinds* of sharing in that single sacrament? Lombard's text was the fundamental starting point for the discussion of this sacrament in the great Scholastics — even to the extent of their treating different aspects of Order in the sequence he had suggested.

What, then, *was* the teaching of the high medieval theologians on this subject? People like Thomas (1225-1274) and Bonaventure (1221-1274) began by situating sacramental order within a theology of order in general — that is, a theology of the way ecclesial society possesses a variety of ministries, and is arranged in a hierarchical pattern. They propose that this ordered variety in the Church is a manifestation of the richness of God's wisdom. It shows the amplitude of that wisdom better than would a flat, 'democratic' equality. Ordered variety multiplies the possibilities of co-operating in diverse ways with the work of salvation. Order, in the general sense of that word, is desirable in the Church so as to express the *ordered way* in which God communicates his own perfections to his creatures. To say this is, naturally, to situate order within not only human society, but the cosmos as a whole — the creation, or, as we still say, the created *order*. It presupposes that there is a chain of being, reaching down from the Good through all levels of created being in the cosmos and that this chain is continued in the ordered structure of human society.[26]

So far, then, nothing has been said about Order in the specific context of Christ and his Gospel. But at this point, the Scholastics note that, in the Christian economy, the ordering principle in the world has a special significance of its own. It is used, in fact, to convey to people the sources of grace — the sacraments. Now in and of itself, this need not necessarily mean that the Church's own ordering principle be sacramental. But, or so Thomas argues in the *Summa contra Gentiles,* it was at any rate highly suitable that order should itself be made into a sacrament. Thomas' reason for saying this is that it is fitting to the generosity of God. It befits God's generous goodness that he did not arrange spiritual functions in the community of his Son without joining to those functions the grace required for their proper exercise.[27]

Convergently, Bonaventure argues that the power to confer other sacraments ought to be itself a sacrament.[28] The high medievals, therefore, could disagree as to why it was appropriate that Order be a sacrament, but none of them disputed that it was so. All agreed with the Master of the Sentences that Order certainly is a sacrament, since by a visible rite it confers not only office but spiritual power, along with the grace desirable for the worthy exercise of its functions.[29]

This bare definition was pondered on and drawn out in various ways. It formed the central affirmation around whose sun six planetary questions revolved. These were: firstly, what is the aim of Order? secondly, what is its consecratory quality or *character*? thirdly, how is it internally differentiated? fourthly, what is the essential rite of ordination? fifthly, who is the minister of this sacrament? sixthly, who is its subject, that is, its proper recipient? Let us take them in turn.

First, then, what is the aim of Order? The purpose of this sacrament is described by the high Scholastics as the communicating to the faithful of the sanctifying influence of Jesus Christ, the Church's head.[30] It is not so much for the benefit of the ordained man himself as for that of the wider Church, indeed, of the whole Church. Such sanctification of human beings, the goal of this sacrament, was frequently further specified by speaking of the New Law or new Covenant instituted by Christ. Theologians pointed out that the central feature of life under that new Covenant, its highest moment, was the Eucharistic sacrifice, whereby the Church shares actively in Christ's death and Resurrection, for the salvation of the world. Thus the central element in the ministerial sanctification of men and women through Order must needs be the Eucharist. As Bonaventure put it succinctly, *ordo est ad sacrificium administrandum,* 'Order is for the ministering of sacrifice'.[31] The preaching of the Word and pastoral government, the prophetic and royal aspects of the apostolic ministry, are ordered to participation in the Eucharist, the central act of its priestly office.

Secondly, what about the consecratory quality or character which results from this sacrament? The conferring of Order is not only a commissioning for a function, and a bestowal of grace for carrying out that function in a Christian fashion. It also entails the permanent consecration of a man, termed by the Scholastics 'character'.[32] The word 'character', meaning originally a mark or stamp, was borrowed from the Greek fathers in order to express what, in the patristic West, Augustine had called the lasting *signaculum* or sign-quality, which this sacrament leaves on those who receive it.[33]

In medieval discussion, stimulated by the work of Lombard, character — whether in baptism, confirmation or Order — was regarded as a reality mid-way between, on the one hand, the visible rite whereby the Church bestows a sacrament, and, on the other, the sacramental grace which the ritual action sets flowing in the recipient. Character has it in common with the visible rite that it is an efficacious sign of grace, while it resembles grace inasmuch as it is an invisible spiritual reality, brought forth and signified by the rite in question.[34] Attempts further to elaborate an understanding of the consecration found in these sacraments started out, frequently enough, from Aristotle's notion of the 'categories', theologians teasing out thereby what *sort of quality* this consecratory effect might be. Gradually a rich doctrine of character, not least for the mystery (it is no less!) of Order, was unfolded.

William of Auxerre (d. 1231) conceived character as a disposition to grace: by marking the soul with this consecratory stamp, God prepares it to receive the grace which will perfect the individual person in that specific way which the sacrament's own symbolic structure lays forth.[35] For Alexander of Hales (c.1170-1245), appealing to the teaching of the Letter to the Hebrews that the Son is the 'character' or figure of the Father's substance, character in the initiated or ordained Christian must be understood christologically — as a configuration to Christ. He by whom the Father created all things is, appropriately enough, the agent through whom God impresses the divine mark on creatures in the supernatural order. To Alexander's mind, while all three sacramental characters configure the person to the redeeming Christ, each has a distinctive relationship to the glorious Cross which is the trophy of his victory. Whereas baptismal character is a sign of faith in the suffering Christ, and the character received in confirmation of courageous profession of Christ's Cross, the ordained character signifies a *compatire,* 'co-sharing', in the redemptive suffering of the God-man. Character thus operates as a sign of that configuration — not just to the Son but to the whole Trinity, each of whom in different ways was at work in the Passion of the Lord — which grace achieves in literal reality.[36]

Thomas Aquinas, too, sees character as a new relationship to Christ.[37] Like the relationships to Christ conferred by baptism and confirmation, this is something more than just psychology. As with the sacraments of initiation, this more than merely psychological reality is a new relationship to Christ as high priest: to Christ, that is, as the mediator between God and man.[38] The high-priesthood of Christ is, after all, an excellent expression for his two-way mediatorial activity, which goes up from man to God in his humanity, and down from God to man in his divinity. Christ as priest is the principle both of all human worship of God, and of all divine sanctification of human beings. And so the permanent consecration, or character, which enables these two kinds of activity — liturgical activity towards the Father, sanctifying activity towards other people — must be a sharing in the high-priesthood of Christ. This is yet another reason for highlighting the term 'priesthood', both in its general application to the Christian laity, and in its special application to the ordained. The character bestowed in baptism and confirmation makes the laity a prophetic and royal priesthood; the character given with Order makes the ordained a ministerial priesthood, though one which — mirroring that of the laity, and derived from that of the apostleship — has prophetic and royal dimensions. Thomas' insistence that character must be understood, essentially, in terms of Christian worship — as a deputation to the *cultus Dei,* the Liturgy, which is at once a mystery of adoration of God, and of sanctification of men, was accepted by the majority of his Scholastic successors.

This 'ontological' understanding of the Church's ministry thus became, with the great Scholastics, part and parcel of the Church's theological — and, with the close of the Middle Ages, at Trent, dogmatic — tradition. The 'inner basis' of that understanding, as one of its contemporaries' guardians, Walter Kasper of Tübingen, has stressed:

> consists in the fact that Jesus Christ, as head and high priest of his Church, is himself the primary proclaimer, distributer of the sacraments and shepherd, who works through the priest and — in borderline cases — even through a bad priest. For many priests who feel unequal to the high claims that their ministry imposes on them — and for what priest would this not be the case? —

precisely this 'ontological' understanding is a help and a consolation, because they can say to themselves that the salvation of their communities and of the people committed to them does not ultimately depend on their own accomplishments and their own success.[39]

And, pointing out that this can be a consolation for their communities too (!), Kasper formulates this conviction in a paradox: because a priest's activity is pure service, it is always more than his own service, 'more than human and Christian praxis'. And in any case the alternatives of function or ontology, mission or character, do not withstand close analysis. It is

> precisely when one understands function ... not (as) being an external function quality but (as) something that draws a person completely into service and seizes him, that one can see how it stamps a person in his very nature and how it is an ontological determination of that person, which does not exist *in addition* to that person's essential relations and functions but rather *in* them. As soon as one frees oneself from a purely substantialist and 'heavy-handed' ontology, which was certainly not the ontology of the great theologians of the High Middle Ages, alternatives like that between ontological and functional disappear of themselves.[40]

Thus, for instance, for Thomas, to be vested with sacramental character is to be charged with an essentially instrumental function (one might well say 'mission') of a ministerial kind.[41]

What, then, of the internal differentiation of this sacrament? The high Scholastics were in agreement that Order is sevenfold. There was an inbuilt tendency to come up with this number, since seven is such a frequent symbol of perfection in the Bible, and in Christian tradition. Most of the medieval divines considered that the episcopate and presbyterate make up together one single order which, naturally enough, they set at the head of their list. We have already noted those features of the patristic landscape which led people along this false trail. The theological consensus in favour of telescoping the two orders of the ministerial priesthood was never, however, all-embracing. From William of Auxerre to Gabriel Biel, important figures stood out against the trend. St Thomas' nuanced position does credit both to his familiarity with the Fathers and to his own instincts. While Aquinas does not call the episcopate a distinct order when discussing Order as a whole, he holds, none the less, an exalted doctrine of the episcopate, comparable to that of Hippolytus and the early Roman church at large. In particular, Thomas was saved from the excesses of the 'presbyterianising' tendency inherited from Jerome by his attention to the liturgical prayers of the Roman rite.

> He speaks of the headship, *principalitas*, of the bishop over the mystical body in a way which shows that it is no mere office of jurisdiction but a genuine spiritual headship. He affirms the bishop's duty to preach as one of his principal obligations, since this is a task to which the apostles gave great importance and the bishop is their successor. The power of the bishop is superior to that of the presbyter in all that concerns the faithful. As ruler of the mystical body he acts in the person of Christ, and he appoints its members officially to the different functions which exist in the body; thus the sacrament of confirmation and the sacrament of order are administered by the bishop. To presbyters, however, he delegates powers for the personal sanctification of the faithful, since it is only right that the head should concern himself with the officers but delegate care for the lesser members to his collaborators. The presbyter receives the sacerdotal character and power over the body of Christ in the Eucharist from ordination, but he receives his power over the mystical body from an episcopal mandate, *ex episcopi commissione.*[42]

Whilst Thomas' account draws too sharp a line between the presbyter's Eucharistic presidency and his other 'powers', notably that of the keys, to be altogether satisfactory, it represents an important testimony to the persistence of the earlier, universal tradition.[43]

Aside from the episcopate-presbyterate, the other six orders recognised by the generality of Scholastic divines were, in descending sequence: deacon, sub-deacon, lector, exorcist, acolyte and door-keeper. So far as the sevenfold structure of Order was concerned, medieval theologians were frequently quite well aware that not all of the seven which they recognised had been conferred independently, or practised separately, in the early Church. Scotus (c.1264-1308) held that the five minor orders were given simultaneously to the presbyter-bishops and deacons of the primitive community.[44] Thomas and Bonaventure say that they were contained implicitly within the diaconate.[45] In point of fact, this latter statement is not so far from the historical truth, in that, as we have seen, minor orders arose as forms of assistance to the deacon in his ministry.

How are the seven Orders arranged? Under the influence of the sixth-century Syrian writer known as the pseudo-Denys, people saw them as a reflection of the seven angelic orders of the angelic hierarchy. Alternatively, they divided them up into three categories, following a scheme, also derived from Denys, of ministers who *purify* (such as exorcists), ministers who *illuminate* (like the deacon, reading the Gospel in the Liturgy), and ministers who *perfect* (like the *sacerdotes,* 'priests', whether presbyters or bishops, who give the Real Presence in holy Communion.[46] But the pre-eminent names among the Scholastics preferred to say that the seven orders should be regarded as seven different ways of being related to the liturgical celebration of the Eucharist. The various orders are, they thought, integral parts of a single unity, inasmuch as six of them involve some kind of share in the seventh, the Eucharistic presidency of the presbyter or bishop.[47]

However, this general consensus about the sevenfold differentiation of Order was by no means complete. Durandus thought that there were only two orders, episcopate and presbyterate: all the rest, including the diaconate, being simply sacramentals.[48]

What, then, was the essential gesture of ordination? As already mentioned in connection with the development of the ordination ritual in the early Church, the medievals normally identified the key moment of ordination as the handing over of the 'tools of one's trade', the *porrectio instrumentorum:* the gospel-book for the deacon, for instance, and the chalice with the paten for the priest. But a minority, more conformably to early tradition, opted for the view that the crucial sacramental gesture was really the laying on of hands.

Whom did they take to be the minister of this sacrament? For the high medieval divines, the sole minister, at any rate for major Orders, was the bishop. The role of presbyters, and of an archdeacon, at ordination services was simply, they argued, to add greater ceremonial richness to the occasion. But it was commonly held that the pope could, if he wished, delegate to presbyters the conferring of minor orders. This exception is instructive, given the predominant medieval view that minor orders are genuinely sacramental, to the point of each having its own consecratory quality, its 'character'. People supported such papal delegation to presbyters of the episcopal duty to ordain by arguing that the pope's 'directive power' — what would now be called his 'universal jurisdiction', being itself ordered to the good of the universal Church, was necessarily greater than that of any other bishop, be he metropolitan, be he patriarch. Indeed, for many of the Scholastics, the power of pastoral government, namely jurisdiction, was something conferred on other bishops by the pope. Just so, they held, the apostles held their governing power — as distinct from their power to teach or to sanctify—through Peter, to whom Christ had promised the keys of the kingdom. There was a danger here that a combination of this view that the Pope was the mediate source of the pastoral office, with the widespread opinion that the episcopate and presbyterate were, fundamentally, one single grade of the sacrament of Order, might have undermined Latin Christianity's grasp of the episcopate as the primary apostolic ministry in the Church. And, in fact, historians have evidence that, at various points in the fourteenth and fifteenth centuries, popes gave to abbots in presbyteral orders the right to ordain priests — an abuse which is something of an embarrassment to Catholic spokespersons — whether *vis-à-vis* the Orthodox and Anglo-Catholics, who hold strongly to the classical view of the episcopate, or, for opposite reasons, *vis-à-vis* Presbyterians.[49]

Who, then, finally, was the subject of ordination? Males only, following the precedents set by such early Christian texts as the (Egyptian) *Apostolic Church Order* of around the year 300. It is sometimes said that the issue of women's ordination is completely open theologically since it has never before received considered discussion in the Church's tradition. But this is not so. The medievals offer four kinds of argument, varying considerably in value, for the non-ordination of women in the Church.[50] First, there was a symbolic argument. The Church, symbolised as feminine, was guided and directed by God through Christ, a mediator who is masculine. The state of being-in-authority in the Church is, therefore, more properly symbolised by men; that of being-subject-to-authority by women. Secondly, there were arguments based on women's supposed emotional instability and their greater timidity and, as it was alleged, proneness to lead others into sin. Such arguments were always in part counter-evidential; their users were obliged to admit that there were exceptions. Some women were more intelligent and competent than many men; and some, like the female martyrs, faced difficulty and danger with great courage.

More cogent were the two remaining kinds of argumentation. For, in the third place, there was reference to Christ's positive determinations in the New Testament. Christ chose no women as apostles. But since he himself initiated the sacraments, and since those sacraments confer the grace they do through a covenant God has made with the Church in Christ, it is the will of Christ that must determine the conditions on which this covenant, and so this sacramental programme, is carried out. Fourthly and finally, in a writer like the Franciscan William of Rubio (b. 1290) we find the interesting argument that women cannot be ordained since, if — *per improbabile* — they could, the Church since the time of the apostles would have committed a monstrous injustice in excluding them from ordination. The Church could not have deprived an entire sex of the ability to receive Orders — something of salvific value both for themselves and for others — if in fact women are capable of being ordained.

It may be of some encouragement to women to know that medieval theologians did not, however, regard the use of reason as absolutely necessary for ordination. However, it was held that, for major orders at least, *honestas*, basic decency, as well as Church canons did require it.

Medieval thinking about Order had, then, its strengths, but also its weaknesses. On the credit side, it had reached a clear conception of how the ordained ministry is sacramental. Order is a sacrament because, through a liturgical rite, the Church, acting in the name of Christ, confers an office, an office bringing with it spiritual power. This power is precisely a ministerial power, for the service of others. This service takes the form of a communication of the sanctifying influence of Christ as Head of the Church. Along with the conferral of office and spiritual power, there is also given the grace to perform the functions of the office, and to exercise the power, in a worthy manner. At the same time, the sacrament brings about a consecration of the minister, analogous to that achieved through the sacraments of initiation. This consecration is for the liturgical service of God and for the service, by sanctification, of the world. It is based, then, on the mediatorship or priesthood of Christ, and so is appropriately described as a new kind of share in that priesthood. By this indelible character, the ordained man is related in a new way to Christ as priest. Thus, according to the Scholastics, the ordering principle which every society needs, and which Christ established in the Church by instituting the apostolic ministry, is not only an arrangement for the administration of the sacraments. It is itself a sacrament.

On the debit side, medieval theologians found it difficult to say how and why the single sacrament of Order is differentiated. On the one hand, the minor orders were often regarded as fully sacramental, though theories as to how they could be termed something instituted by Christ ranged from the whimsical to the sophisticated — as in the idea that, in the development of ordained ministry, the Church had 'unfolded' offices implicit in the episcopate, presbyterate or deaconate. On the other hand, episcopate and presbyterate were often lumped together as a single order, with two 'dignities'. This problem stemmed, of course, from the general tendency of the post-Nicene Church to delegate episcopal functions to the presbyters of local congregations, thus giving them the status of mini-bishops. This made it possible to see the presbyterate, not the episcopate, as the essential order in the Church. Combined with the medieval theory that the bishop's power of pastoral government, as distinct from his power to teach and sanctify, is received from the pope, one might have foreseen the evolution of the Latin church into a kind of papal presbyterianism. However, other sources like the Liturgy and the canonists preserved the idea that the episcopate was divinely instituted — in other words, was that ordained ministry into which the apostolic ministry had essentially passed — even when professional theologians were hesitant.[51]

It is a moot point whether the tendency of medieval theology to define Order in terms of relationship to the Eucharist should be termed a weakness or a strength. Although the ministry of the Word is often conspicuous by its absence in medieval definitions of Order, ministerial preaching was understood as preparing people for a share in the Eucharist banquet and sacrifice. To see preaching or the ministry of the Word as finding its climax in Eucharistic participation is to reflect the structure of the Eucharistic liturgy itself, as we find it in all the historic Christian traditions. Analogously, the other sacraments administered by bishop or presbyter can be seen as ordered to the Eucharist — for instance, the anointing of the sick aims at removing a bodily obstacle to sharing in the Mass, while penance removes a moral or spiritual obstacle.

In the next chapter, we must look at what the Reformers made of the achievements of medieval theology, and its lacunae, on this subject, and at the response they in turn elicited from the Catholic side. Meanwhile, however, we may note that, in the creation of a theology of the sacramental character of the ordained, the Middle Ages would pass on to the future a distinctive and enduring contribution very much their own. The Second Vatican Council would not hesitate to re-appropriate that teaching in its own work.

4

The Reformers and the Council of Trent

Despite the achievements of the medieval theology of Order, both that theology and the organisation of the ordained ministry which it presupposed came under increasing fire in the late medieval Church. First, there were anti-clerical groups which espoused a somewhat simplistic egalitarian view of the Church community.[1] Thus, around 1500, Hussite groups in Bohemia were withdrawing from the Church on the grounds that, by accepting the differentiation of the Christian people into a multiplicity of different orders and dignities, it had transgressed the commandment of Jesus in Matthew 23:8: 'call no one on earth your father, for you are all brothers'.[2] This notion, that a diversity of ministries within the body of Christ is incompatible with Gospel brotherhood, is already found in the thirteenth-century *Fraticelli*, spiritual anarchists, who originated among the radical wing of the Franciscans.[3]

The origins of this idea are complex. At one level, it was a protest against the wealth and pomp of the late medieval episcopate. At another level, it drew on an underground anti-sacramental element in religious culture. Originally Oriental, the bearers of this element had spread an attitude of hostility to the material realm, as a vehicle of salvation, from the Middle East, through the Balkans, into Western Europe, taking different names as they did so: Paulicians, Bogomils, Cathars.[4] Modern historians tend to agree with medieval heresiologists that this anti-sacramental element which, quite logically, attacked the sacrament of Order as all others, derives ultimately from outside Christianity in Manichaeanism. But in the West, at least by the late Middle Ages, it had lost its metaphysical character, and become simply a vehicle for lay protest against abuses of ministerial authority, real or imagined.[5] Additionally, mysticism, whilst taking many perfectly orthodox forms, could also be used as justification for 'rejecting the authority of the Church in favour of the authority found within'.[6] This was so among elements of the Beguines (female) and Beghards (male) of the later Middle Ages: groups comparable, perhaps, to the 'secular institutes' of today, though without a clear ecclesiastical sanction. It took on a radically heterodox, indeed pantheistic, form in the movement known as the heresy of the Free Spirit.[7] Finally, there was apocalypticism, which, fuelled by such speculation about future history and the end of time as that provided by the influential south Italian abbot Joachim of Fiore (c.1132-1202), looked forward to a third age of salvation history, following those of the Father (the Old Testament, with its prophecies) and the Son (the New Testament, with its Church of sacraments), and consisting in a purified community of contemplatives who would need no mediators between God and man. The sect known as 'The Apostles', and to their opponents the *pseudo-Apostolici,* is an example of such apocalyptically based anti-sacerdotalism.[8]

Such groups were the natural recruiting ground for followers of the second kind of late medieval critic of the theology and practice of Order. This second category of critic was the professional theologian who, by interpreting Scripture in a different fashion from that usual in the medieval Church, arrived at doctrinal conclusions incompatible with the idea of sacramental Order. The earliest of these was John Wyclif (c.1329-84).[9] Born at Richmond, Yorkshire, about 1330, Wyclif spent most of his life teaching in the theological schools at Oxford. Protected by powerful patrons, especially the Duke of Lancaster, Wyclif was fortunate in that his working life coincided with the beginning of the great Schism in the church of the West, which effectively disabled the Papacy from moving against him. However, in 1381-2, the combination of a commission of Oxford University, and a synod called by the Archbishop of Canterbury, William of Courtenay, meeting at the Oxford Blackfriars, proscribed a number of propositions from his writings, and made the teaching of its doctrine subject to excommunication. Twenty years after his death, the Council of Constance (1414-15), aware of the diffusion of his ideas both in England and central Europe, condemned him as a heresiarch, an act which led eventually to the exhumation of his corpse from its grave at his parish, Lutterworth in Leicestershire, and its unceremonious depositing in a local stream. Where Order was concerned, Wyclif accepted that at least two grades of it, the presbyterate and the diaconate, were known to the primitive Church. The episcopate, however, had been introduced, he thought, through *superbia,* 'arrogance', when ambitious presbyters wanted more power for themselves.[10] Except for this rather jaundiced account of the origins of the episcopate, this general position was, as we have seen, not unusual in its period. What *was* unusual, indeed revolutionary, was the way in which Wyclif applied to ecclesiology, and notably to Order, the Church's teaching on predestination. According to Wyclif, a presbyter or deacon foreknown by God to be reprobate — on the way to damnation — forms no part of the Church. Such an ordained minister has no spiritual power from Christ: his office is a masquerade. Although not denying, therefore, that Order as a twofold ministry is divinely instituted, Wyclif believed that the question, Who exercises this ministry? can be answered only by God. Needless to say, if this be the correct account of the relation of the doctrine of predestination to the doctrine of ecclesiology and sacramental Orders then the Church, as an ordered society, instituted for the communication of grace, can no longer exist.

The same constellation of ideas recurs with Jan Hus who was born in Husinek, in south-west Bohemia, around 1369.[11] After a meteoric rise in the University of Prague he was made, in 1402, rector of the Bethlehem chapel, a centre founded some ten years previously by a member of the merchant class to provide vernacular preaching for the citizens of the Bohemian capital. His campaign for Church reform led to his burning as a heretic by the majority Conciliarist party at the Council of Constance in 1414. Whether he was a Wyclifite, or whether he simply used some of Wyclif's ideas in a rhetorical fashion so as to prosecute his plans for a (largely moral) reform of the life of the Church in general, and of the priesthood in particular, remains a disputed question. The bull *Inter cunctas* of 1416, which attempted to realise the decisions of the Council of Constance, thought it proper, at any rate, to administer to the followers not only of Wyclif but also of Hus, and Hus' disciple Jerome of Prague (c.1370–1416), the question:

> Do you think that an evil-living *(malus)* priest, when using the appropriate matter and form, and intending to do what the Church does, truly confects [the Eucharist], truly absolves, truly baptises, truly confers the other sacraments?[12]

Such doctrinal tests are necessarily terse, for they must pinpoint some tenet vital to the faith and practice of the Church. Had the authors of this particular one wished to offer at the same time a spot of theological inspiration, they could not have done better than turn to a beautiful text of Gregory of Nazianzen which compares the priest to a ring bearing the seal of Christ. Whether the ring is of gold or iron, the impression made in the wax is the same. Thus, whatever the personal holiness of the priest, the effect produced in the sacraments he ministers is all one, since it is the same Christ acting through him.[13]

The wider significance of Hussitism for the Church's history lies mainly in the alliance which it established between the emergent nationalism of late medieval Europe and hostility to the inherited forms of the ordained ministry. In this way, it forms a bridge between Wyclif and the Protestant Reformation.

Much more serious than Hussitism in its long-term consequences was the reception accorded in Germany to Martin Luther's use of the principle of justification by faith alone — itself the centre of his own spiritual strivings. As Luther saw things, if it is faith alone that justifies, then the sacraments cannot be causes of sanctifying grace. They can only be attestations of our faith in God's assurance that he will give us his grace and, indeed, has already done so, forgiving us our sins in Jesus Christ. Luther, in his *Manifesto to the Nobility of the German Nation,* pointed out that all are priests by baptism, sharing the royal and prophetic priesthood of all believers. In itself, of course, this affirmation is perfectly compatible with the acceptance of a ministerial or ordained priesthood. But in his treatise *On the Babylonian Captivity of the Church,* Luther denied that Order, considered as a sacrament, is founded on Scripture. Ordination was, rather, an ecclesiastical ceremony, somewhat like the blessing of vessels for the Holy Communion — his own comparison.[14] And yet, Luther did not propose the abolition of the ordained ministry, after the manner of the medieval anarchist groups, but only its re-interpretation. He considered a pastoral office to have been part-and-parcel of the primitive Church, and to remain necessary for the good order of the continuing community.[15] Essentially, he concluded, ministry comprises two elements: vocation and election. Vocation, to serve the community as a minister of Word and sacraments, comes from God; election comes from the people, who then confer on the individual whose vocation they recognise that degree of ministerial authority they think fit. As Luther's able theological disciple Philip Melanchthon (1497-1560) would explain, a person who is called or elected by those who have the right to call or elect him is already a minister of the Gospel, even without the laying-on of hands. Not that such laying-on of hands was done away with in the Lutheran liturgy. It remained, but as a declaration, simply, of the candidate's vocation.[16]

However, Lutheranism early became much less radical on this issue, in part by way of reaction to still more heterodox groups springing up to its left. Thus, Melanchthon, in his *Loci communes,* declared himself willing to count Order as a sacrament so long as its ministry of Word and sacrament was not taken to include the offering of sacrifice for the living and the dead (for this was a view of the Eucharist remarkably resistant to combination with the Lutheran 'by faith alone').[17] In his *Defence of the Augsburg Confession,* Melanchthon, though uncompromising on this point, regards the inherited ministerial order as rendered venerable by long-standing custom, and to be preserved on grounds of the public good of the Church. Only the non-cooperation of the Catholic episcopate with the Reform prevents the latter's supporters from keeping that order whole and entire. Their desire to safeguard Gospel truth must be their defence to posterity. Whilst the notion that the sacramental priesthood takes its rise from delegation by the spiritual priesthood, the laity, vitiates Melanchthon's account of the ordained ministry at a fundamental level, his more specific doctrine of the episcopal office is wholly traditional in the responsibilities it ascribes to the bishop in his church.[18]

This 'more in sorrow than in anger' approach to the rejection of the apostolic succession of the Church persisted in the Lutheran tradition at large, as may be seen by consulting the Schmalkaldic articles of 1537. For, according to this text, were the ministerial order, as found in the papal Church, genuinely evangelical in its doctrine and practice, then Reformed candidates would willingly seek ordination in continuity with it — in the apostolic succession. But those in Catholic orders are not evangelical, either in mind or behaviour. For they neither accept the doctrine of justification by faith alone, seen as the heart of the Gospel, nor do they live as though that doctrine were true. They are, therefore, a pseudo-ministry, and the Church, which is the fundamental bearer of apostolicity, thus returns of necessity to its primitive condition: congregational self-government by the calling, choosing and ordaining of fresh pastors.[19]

This was also Jean Calvin's (1509-64) view in Book Four of his *Institutes of the Christian Religion,* in which he poured some well-informed scorn on the confusing variableness of Scholastic opinions about the number of holy Orders and the relation between them. As a controversialist, Calvin does not in general exhibit the violence which mars Luther's work, yet the section of the *Institutes* which deals with Order is called, uncompromisingly enough, 'On the five falsely so-called sacraments'.[20] The inability of Catholic theologians to agree just how many grades of Order there are is, for Calvin, a give-away symptom of the fact that they are disputing about divine things without the Word of God. It is, he maintains, absurd to suppose that the Holy Spirit consecrates such office-holders as door-keepers who keep no doors and exorcists who never attempt to exorcise. In any case, they were unknown to the early Church, a fact which of itself disqualifies them from sacramental status, since only Jesus Christ himself could institute an authentic sacrament. The claim of the Catholic priesthood to exercise a reconciling role between God and man makes out the one sacrifice of Christ to be insufficient for salvation; that priesthood is, therefore, Godless and sacrilegious. Although Christ filled his disciples with the Holy Spirit, the notion that the apostolic laying-on of hands, with anointing, does the same is falsified by daily experience. Catholic priests are, rather, successors of the Levites of Judaism, and in this they renege on Christ and deny the office of a Christian pastor. Indeed, Calvin accuses the Catholic Church of making a *potpourri* of Christianity, Judaism and paganism. The laying-on of hands is, in certain cases, an effective sign of God's grace — but only for those who obey Christ's commandments and seek to fulfil the actual purpose for which the ministry was created. Nor do deacons fare better than the bishops and presbyters against whom Calvin thus inveighs. The apostolic Church possessed a diaconate, but the functions ascribed to Catholic deacons, and their rite of ordination, differ from the genuine diaconate as chalk from cheese.

As this account suggests, Calvin did not, any more than Luther, propose to do away with an ordained ministry in his Reformed congregations. The apostles instituted pastors, teachers and deacons by the laying on of hands. At one level, this gesture is simply a symbol: it serves to bring home to the people the value of the ministerial office, and to remind the ordained that he is now obligated to God and the Church. But at another level, the symbol can be itself efficacious in the order of grace; it is, in its way, sacramental, though it is only so when those who ordain and those who are ordained share an authentically evangelical — that is, Reformed! — understanding of faith.[21]

As usual where matters ecclesiological are concerned, the standpoint of the third most influential Reformer, Huldrych Zwingli (1484-1531), is distinctly 'lower' that that of Luther and Calvin.[22] For Zwingli, the only Christian sense that can be given to the term 'priest' is that of proclaimer of the Word of God. The liturgical office of the bishop or the presbyter, which in the Catholic view, comes to its climax in the offering of the Eucharistic sacrifice, is an offence to Christ the High Priest, who, being eternal, can have no successors to his priesthood. However, Zwingli does allow that activities other than simply preaching can 'belong to the Word of God' and so be suitably attached to the office of a pastor. These include healing, visiting the sick, helping the poor and giving alms to them, and — a peculiar stress of the Zurich reformer's — translating the Hebrew and Greek of the original biblical texts, an activity which, Zwingli believed, was the job of the first Christian 'prophets' as mentioned in Ephesians. Zwingli's two main accounts of the ministry of the Word come in two sermons, 'The Shepherd' of 1524 and 'The Ministry' of 1525. The first is directed against Catholicism, and attacks the bad pastor who preaches his own ideas rather than God's Word, or, if he *does* teach God's Word does not act to the glory of God. The second is directed against the extreme left wing of the Reformation, the Anabaptists, and argues that Christ instituted a pastorate in his Church, a single ministry with four aspects, pastoring, evangelising, teaching and prophesying. No one can take this office on himself, but must be commissioned to it by a church: here Zwingli hoped to defend the idea of an orderly, educated (and salaried) ministry over against itinerant anabaptist preachers.

What all these accounts — Luther's, Calvin's, Zwingli's — have in common is that they play off the Word of God in Scripture against living tradition as represented by the apostolic ministry. They exalt the first over the second so as to produce a kind of Protestant Donatism: it is not the ordained minister's public sins that nullify his ordination, but his departure from the Word of God embodied in the Bible. To be able to exercise this criterion presupposes that the Word of God in Scripture can be identified without the assistance of the apostolic ministry. It testifies to what has been called the 'exegetical optimism' of early Protestantism, in other words, the belief that the plain sense of Scripture was in itself something relatively easy to grasp.[23] Good exegesis chases out bad, leaving the evangelical nakedness of false ministers exposed for all the Church to see.

English-speaking readers may be expected to evince a particular interest in that unique product of this turbulent period, Anglicanism. Where Order is concerned:

> The sixteenth century documents of the Church of England concerning the ordained ministry reflect in a remarkable degree the familiar truth that in England the battle between Reformation and Counter-Reformation was not fought to the finish.[24]

Though retaining the threefold structure of the ministry (bishops, priests, deacons) and conserving, in the words of commission to a new presbyter, the handing on of a 'power of the keys' as found in the Latin pontificals, Thomas Cranmer's (1489-1556) *Ordinal* removed all reference to a priest's duty to offer the Eucharistic sacrifice for the living and the dead, replacing the giving of chalice and paten with the gift of a bible. Most Catholic commentators since have regarded the English Reformation as rupturing the transmission of the apostolic ministry on dual grounds: defect of *intention,* and defect of *form.* Defect of intention because 'a positive act of will against an essential feature of the sacrament (viz. in this case, the creation of a Eucharistic ministry of consecration and sacrifice) necessarily vitiates the whole intention and so invalidates the sacrament';[25] defect of form because the distinctive nature of the ministries of presbyter and bishop was insufficiently determined in the new rites. It was on these counts that, in 1897, the bull *Apostolicae curae* of Pope Leo XIII would confirm the entirely consistent Catholic practice since Cranmer of unconditionally ordaining Anglican ministers who might have liked to continue their pastoral office in the new circumstances of full communion with the Church. Since that time, the role of Old Catholic consecrators at some Anglican ordinations, and the adoption of revised ordination rituals constitute new factors, themselves counter-balanced, however, in terms of the general acceptability of the Anglican ministry to Catholics, by the decision of Anglicans to admit women to diaconate, presbyterate and episcopate. Moreover, the earliest grounds alleged by Catholics for the invalidity of Anglican Orders concern departure from the orthodox faith (a 'Cyprianic' rather than 'Augustinian' argument), and the doctrinal security of the faith of the 'undivided Church' in present-day Anglicanism is far from clear even to sympathetic observers.

Between 1517 and 1562 a number of individual Catholic theologians attempted a response to the Reformers by way of defence of the sacrament of Order as understood and practised in the Church. Especially influential was St John Fisher's (1469-1535) *Defence of the Sacred Priesthood against Luther* which ran through five editions between its publication in 1525 and the opening of the Council of Trent. Fisher appeals first of all to the immemorial practice of those churches which recognise the orthodox Fathers. This he terms 'the prescriptive right of existing truth'.[26] Secondly, he considers, through the medium of this patristic tradition, the Scriptural witness itself, before proceeding to a point-by-point rebuttal of Luther's case. Fisher's fundamental approach is Tertullianic in that, like the ancient North African writer, he aimed to show that his adversaries, by deviating from what the apostolic churches had received, had lost their rights to plead in a Christian process:

> If it were ever suitable to use the argument of prescription against any heretic on behalf of any doctrine, never could it be more justly used against Luther in defence of the truth of the priesthood ... Let Luther discover, if he can, any church in the whole world, founded by one of the apostles or one of their followers, which does not possess the priesthood.[27]

In his approach to Scripture, Fisher shows how the apostolic ministry is perpetuated in the churches of the later New Testament period by the laying-on of hands, and he supports his exegesis by arguing for the antecedent probability that in matters concerning salvation, some would be set apart to act in the name of, and bear responsibility for, the many.

A Dominican writer may be forgiven for drawing attention also to the extensive, but little studied, early defences of this sacrament offered by a member of the Order of Preachers in the German lands. Johannes Mensing's *Oration on the Priesthood of Christ's Catholic Church,* and its companion piece *Examination of the Texts and Arguments Adduced by Martin Luther against the Priesthood of the Church in his Book about the Abrogation of the Mass,* both appeared in 1527.[28] The friar from Saxony, who died as *Weihbischof* (auxiliary bishop) of Halberstadt in 1541, had been recognised a year earlier, at the Disputation of Worms, as one of the leading Catholic spokesmen in the German church. He departed from his usual vernacular style to address the clergy of Magdeburg in two Latin orations, regarded as sufficiently valuable to be republished as late as 1685. In the first book, Mensing anticipates Trent in seeing in the apostolate the visible *sacerdotium* of Christ's Church — dispensers of the mysteries of God, and he points out, over against Luther's account of the ministry as, in the concrete, generated by popular election that it is, rather, from God in Christ via the original apostolic leaders. In the second book, these points are developed with the aid of fuller biblical and patristic materials. Like Luther (paradoxically), Mensing is, above all, an exegete of the Paul whom he describes as 'holy leader, ... judge, teacher and rector of the churches'. The sacrament of Order was treated more briefly in many of the manuals of controversial theology of these years following hard on the outbreak of Luther's revolt. But anything like a considered consensual or corporate response had to await not simply the convocation of the Council of Trent, but the painful progress which brought it at last to the disputed question of Order in its twenty-third session.[29]

After a variety of postponements, the Council of Trent finally opened on 13 December 1545. The principal preliminary, whether the Council should first discuss dogma or disciplinary reform, was settled by the compromise that the subjects should be treated concurrently. Trent adopted the procedure of first submitting texts for discussion to gatherings of theologians, known as 'congregations'. These meetings, having sifted their materials, passed on the result to the bishops, who were the actual voting members of the Council. On Order, seven articles were submitted to such congregations and the opinion of the theologians present was sought as to their erroneous quality and on whether or not they should be formally anathematised.

They were:
1. Order is not a sacrament. It is simply a rite which consists in choosing and instituting ministers of the Word and sacraments.
2. Not only is Order not a sacrament, it is a fiction, invented by men who are ignorant in theological matters.
3. Order is not a single sacrament. The minor and intermediate orders are not *gradus,* 'grades' or 'ranks', tending towards the order of priesthood.
4. There is no hierarchy in the Church. All Christians are equally priests. For the use or exercise of this priesthood, there is needed choice by civil authority, *magistratus,* and consent by the people. The person who is thus ordained can return to being a simple layman.
5. In the new Covenant, there is not given any visible, public priesthood, nor any spiritual power, whether to consecrate the Lord's Body and Blood, or to offer it, or to absolve sins before God. There exists only a function, whose aim is the preaching of the Gospel. Those who do not preach the Gospel are not truly priests.
6. Not only is anointing not required in the conferring of Orders. It is positively harmful, and should be rejected, as should all other ceremonies. In ordination, the Holy Spirit is not given. Thus bishops commit an affront when saying to ordinands, Receive the Holy Spirit.

7. Bishops are not higher than presbyters. They have no right to ordain ministers, or, if they have such a right, they have it in common with presbyters. Ordinations which they perform without the consent of the faithful are void.[30]

These articles, though they represent the views of no single Reformed figure, offer a fair overview of the positions bruited in dissident circles. The Council, then, did not attack a straw man: it was familiar with the genuine opinions of its adversaries.

After a somewhat complex process of discussion and revision, there emerged from these articles the final text of what the conciliar fathers of Trent wished to say in response. Promulgated in July 1563, their document started out from the relation between Order and the Eucharist.[31] Not only was this a commonplace of medieval theology, it also provided a link with the twenty-second session of the Council, which had been devoted to the Eucharistic sacrifice. In chapter one (*DS* 1764) of the Decree, then, the Council of Trent teaches that the Eucharist, the sacrifice of the New Covenant, is so intimately connected to the sacrament of Order that the one cannot be imagined as existing without the other. To make possible the celebration of the Eucharist, Christ instituted a sacramental priesthood in the person of his apostles, and this priesthood is continued in their successors. The Council deliberately forebore from attempting to describe the process by which this apostolic priesthood was so instituted.

In chapter two (*DS* 1765) the ministry attached to the priesthood is said to be a divine gift, to ensure whose worthy exercise the Church has attached to the priesthood *plures et diversi ... ministrorum ordines* ('a number of different ministerial orders'), so that those who exercise major orders may approach them by appropriate stages. Trent was undecided as to whether the sub-diaconate should count as a major order, contenting itself in the end with pointing out that a number of Church fathers and early Councils speak as though it were so.

In chapter three (*DS* 1766), the fathers of Trent insist that Order is itself truly a sacrament, appealing here to Scripture, to apostolic tradition and to the patristic consensus. Leaving open the question as to what precisely is the crucial sacramental gesture in the bestowal of Order, they speak of it, quite simply, as accomplished by means of words and gestures which confer grace.

In chapter four (DS 1767-1769), the Council affirms the permanence of the consecration that Order brings about. It also declares that the bishops are the principal members of the ministerial hierarchy, since they have succeeded to the apostles as governors of the Church of God — with a reference to Paul's farewell speech at Ephesus in Acts 20. However, this chapter is very carefully worded, since the Tridentine bishops did not wish to define the divine origin of the superiority of the episcopate to the presbyterate — something which was left to their successors at the Second Vatican Council to achieve. In what is perhaps its strongest passage, the text denounces the creation of ministers by a combination of civil authority and the people. Those who, through their own temerity, assume the ordained ministry must be regarded not as the Church's members but — with a reference to John 10 — as thieves and robbers who have not entered by the gate. The 'gate' is, evidently, the apostolic succession, whereby the original apostolic mandate is continued sacramentally over time.

No full account of Trent's teaching on Order is possible, however, without searching the decrees of the Council for references to the priesthood in other contexts. The effect of such a search is to broaden the picture of Order which results, to see with Trent that Order occupies a wider circle than that inscribed by the demands of the Eucharistic sacrifice alone. Obvious places to look are passages on the other sacraments: since, of some of these, bishops and priests are the only celebrants, as in penance and the anointing of the sick, or they are the normal celebrants, as in baptism, or at the least they play a major part, as in marriage. Even more productive is consulting the decrees on Church reform, scattered as these are through the twenty-five sessions of the Council. Examination of the decrees on reform shows how strongly

Trent insisted on the prophetic office attached to the apostolic ministry. Thus, in session V, for example, the decree on reform calls the preaching of the Gospel 'the principal duty of bishops'. And it goes on to say of priests:

> Archpriests, curates and all those who in any manner soever hold any parochial, or other, churches, which have the cure of souls, shall, at least on the Lord's days, and solemn feasts either personally, or if they be lawfully hindered, by others who are competent, feed the people committed to them, with wholesome words, according to their own capacity, and that of their people; by teaching them the things which it is necessary for all to know unto salvation, and by announcing to them with briefness and plainness of discourse, the vices which they must avoid, and the virtues which they must follow after, that they may escape everlasting punishment, and obtain the glory of heaven.[32]

The same decree lays down censures against priests with the *cura animarum* who fail to preach — as well as against those who preach heretically, though in the latter case it advises bishops to proceed against them with caution, for fear of committing injustice. The decree also requires bishops to institute suitably qualified priests to lectureships in theology, understood as the exposition of Scripture, one for every cathedral and every collegiate church in each large town.

The Council returned to the topic of preaching in session XXIV, extending the provisions it had laid down earlier. A further decree on reform required parish priests to preach daily during Lent and Advent, or at the least on three days in the week 'if ... the bishops shall deem it needful, and, at other times, as often as they shall judge that it can be opportunely done'. The bishops moreover:

> shall diligently admonish the people, that each one is bound to be present at his own parish church, where it can be conveniently done, to hear the Word of God.[33]

Trent also required bishops and parish priests to exercise the ministry of the Word whenever a sacrament was administered. The aim was 'that the faithful people may approach the reception of the sacraments with greater reverence and devotion of mind'. This is still of importance today. As the contemporary liturgical composer André Gouze, OP, has written, 'All rite without preaching becomes magic; every word without rite turns into propaganda and ideology.'[34] To achieve this goal, they are to explain to the people 'the efficacy and use of those sacraments'. For this purpose, the Council commissioned a catechism, which was to be translated into the vernacular and expounded by the parish clergy, the better to impress on all hearts the meaning of the 'sacred oracles', that is, the Bible, and the 'maxims of salvation': presumably, the rule of faith found in tradition.[35]

If we turn, then, to the Catechism of the Council of Trent, we find that the sacrament of Order is itself one of the sacraments whose Christian sense is thus to be expounded. While relatively few people would witness ordination ceremonies, which were largely confined to cathedrals, it was too important to pass over in silence. As the Catechism explains:

> From an attentive consideration of the nature and properties of the other sacraments, we shall find little difficulty in perceiving, that so dependent are they all on the sacrament of Order that without its intervention some could not at all be consecrated or administered; whilst others should be stripped of the religious rites and solemn ceremonies, and of that exterior respect, which accompany their administration. The pastor, therefore, following up his exposition of the Sacraments, will deem it a duty to bestow also the greater attention on the sacrament of Order.[36]

The authors of the Catechism predict that preaching about Order will help the pastor himself, who in this way will stir up the grace he received at his own ordination. It will inspire

others who may be proceeding to Orders with a renewed piety
and understanding; and it will show the faithful why honour
is due to the Church's ministers as well as suggesting to
individuals among them the possibility of a vocation.

Not surprisingly, given what we have seen of the reform
decrees of Trent, the Catechism, in its model exposition of
Order, speaks first and foremost of the prophetic office. Bishop
and priest are *tanquam Dei interpretes et internuncii,* 'as it were
the interpreters and heralds of God'. For they are commissioned
to teach mankind *divinam legem et vitae praecepta:* the 'divine law',
faith, and the 'precepts of life', morals. Turning to the priestly
office properly so called, the Catechism finds in that office the
chief ground of the unique place of episcopate and presbyterate
in the Church. As it puts it:

> The power of consecrating and offering the Body and
> Blood of our Lord, and of remitting sins, with which the
> priesthood of the New Law is invested, transcends human
> reason and intelligence. It is not equalled by, or like,
> anything else on earth.[37]

The Catechism is clear that all members of the Church are called
to holiness, what it terms 'the pursuit of piety and innocence',
but it finds that this does not diminish the specialness of those
who are 'initiated in the sacrament of Order', with special duties
to discharge, special functions to perform'.[38]

Perhaps the main distinctive contribution of the Catechism
to the totality of the Tridentine reform, where priesthood is
concerned, lies in its stress on the spiritual qualifications of the
would-be priest. It speaks, in tones learnt, it may be, from the
president of its board of drafters, St Robert Bellarmine
(1542-1621), of the ordinand's need for holiness of life, for
an outstanding grasp of the realities of revelation, for faith,
and for prudence. Whilst the conciliar decrees themselves, to
be sure, are concerned with the quality both of the ordained
and of ordinands, they express this more in terms of worthiness
and competence than in those of holiness. But the Catechism's
stress on the holiness which priests should possess, its *esprit*

exalté on this subject when compared with the sobriety of the conciliar texts themselves, was an anticipation of the future.

Eight doctrinal canons were attached to this decree of Trent on Order (*DS* 1771-1778). They anathematise those who reject its main doctrinal affirmations. Of some theological importance is the eighth doctrinal canon, which anathematises those who maintain that bishops selected by the Roman pontiff are not true bishops. This canon carefully refrains from anathematising those who deny that the bishop's governing authority derives from the pope as the Church's supreme pastor — which left the way open for a nuanced account of this point at the Second Vatican Council. The eighteen disciplinary canons also raise points of interest. They aim at restoring the role of the bishop in the local church to something like its pre-Nicene dimensions. The bishop is to remain physically in his diocese; he is to preach regularly in his cathedral; he is to oversee at first hand the exercise of all other ministries in the local church; he is not to promote anyone to any degree of the sacrament of Order unless the necessity or utility of his church demands it.[39]

> The Council meant to put a distance between the holy Orders and those only too numerous individuals who saw in ordination nothing more than an instrument of their own family interest, and sought to be ordained in a way that failed to respect either the needs of the Church or their suitability.[40]

These canons, together with the relevant sections of the decrees on reform, and the Tridentine catechism, provided a new pastoral ideal for the post-Tridentine bishop, and soon spiritual writers such as Luis of Granada (1505-1588) found themselves invited to flesh it out with an 'episcopal spirituality'.[41] The Catholic reform owes much to the vision of those who saw, and communicated, a sense of the full spiritual dimensions of the bishop's office: thus the Dominican Bartholomew de Martyribus (1514-90), Archbishop of Braga in Portugal, in persuading the young St Charles Borromeo (1538-84) that asceticism and devotion could find no higher expression than in pastoral duties set the latter on the path that would eventually make him the acclaimed archetype of what a bishop should be.[42]

The last of the disciplinary canons is also most important for the later formation, and image, of the presbyter. It declared the appropriate place of formation for the ordained ministry to be the seminary — an institution which seems to have originated in various places at more or less the same time, in the course of the Catholic 'pre-reform' of the early sixteenth century, and is here given what has proved its permanent place in the organisational fabric of the Church.[43] Hitherto, the education of the clergy had been a somewhat hit-and-miss affair. In the patristic period, boys or young men would be attached to the service of a given church, assisting the bishop and presbyters in their duties, and learning thereby how to read and explain the Scriptures, how to prepare catechumens for baptism, and to administer the sacraments. In some places, candidates lived in the bishop's house: as in the case of Eusebius of Vercelli (d.371), described approvingly by Ambrose.[44] Augustine's example, and the influence of his *Rule,* encouraged such a practice.[45] In the West from the seventh to mid twelfth centuries, the predominant locus of learning for deacon and priest had been, however, the monastic or episcopal school. These were in turn displaced by the rise of the medieval university system, though only a fraction of ordinands would ever have graduated from these great academic centres of Latin Christendom. Colleges at such universities as Oxford and Cambridge were nevertheless in a number of cases dedicated specifically to clerical training: indeed, one of the earliest known uses of the term *seminarium* is in John Fisher's statutes for Christ's College, Cambridge.[46] The immediate background to the establishment — at least in principle — of the seminary system by Trent was, more specifically, the founding of the experimental, but highly successful, German College at Rome, and the efforts of Cardinal Reginald Pole (1500–1558) at the reform synod of London of 1555, designed to restore the Catholic Church in England in the wake of the Henrician and

Edwardine reformations, to create in each diocese a 'seed-bed' *(seminarium)* for future priests, under the bishop's guardianship and with the best teachers that money could buy.[47] It would take time before the Tridentine decrees, in this as in other respects, achieved anything as adventurous as enactment — such were the forces of vested interest and inertia. Nor, though I have used the word 'system', were the bodies to which it led anything like monochrome. As Père Marie-Humbert Vicaire, OP, has pointed out: whereas the French *grand' seminaire* joined 'sacred studies' to practical preparation and spiritual formation in a single programme, in the German-speaking countries the 'seminary', strictly so-called, was often reduced to just a few months of pastoral training, ordinands studying in the university faculties and, during their academic year, living in 'hostels', *Konvikten,* run with the spirit of the seminaries elsewhere.

> Doubtless the University system, closer to that of the Middle Ages, forms, in general, a more learned clergy, better informed on contemporary scholarship. The system of the seminaries produces a more religious priesthood. Yet *au fond* the contrast is not that startling. These are not two contradictory formulae, but two conditions of the same institution: the seminary issued from the canons of the Council.[48]

Since the Council had not indicated how such seminaries should be structured and run, their creation was anything but smooth. As with the picture of the ideal bishop, whilst Trent had provided valuable cues, it did not offer a fully-fledged presbyteral spirituality: the portrait of the spiritual priest, clothed with ministerial holiness, remained to be painted.[49] Whereas Charles Borromeo, once again, was a pioneer in episcopal solicitude for the formation of the presbyterate, the making of this portrait had to await the appearance of the post-Tridentine 'French School', to which we shall shortly turn.

What we may here note as emerging from the work of Trent is, above all, the concept of the priest as the 'man of the Mass'.

Whilst, as we have seen, the Tridentine fathers do not present the sacrament of Order so exclusively, so unilaterally, in terms of the Eucharist as has sometimes been alleged, there can be little doubt of the centrality of the Mass to their understanding of the ordained ministry.[50] Their successors, the bishops of the Second Vatican Council, will re-affirm that the offering of the Holy Mysteries in the eucharistic *synaxis* is indeed the climax of a presbyter's whole work.

5

From the Council of Trent to the Catholic Revival

The most important immediately post-Tridentine theologian of the sacrament of Order was the president of the commission on the Catechism, Bellarmine.[1] The Jesuit ecclesiologist stressed two points which would certainly find a place in a sound theology of this sacrament. And these were, first, the affirmation that the essential gesture of conferring the sacrament is the laying-on of hands, and, secondly, the claim that, in what is thus given by God to the candidate for the Church, the difference between the episcopate and the presbyterate is itself a sacramental distinction, and not just a matter of an ecclesiastical decision to give more powers, within Christ's mystical body, to one minister rather than another.[2]

Bellarmine, though learned, has his limitations as a 'positive' theologian, and the historical evidence for these two theses had to be provided rather later, by his fellow Jesuit, Denis Pétau, or Petavius (1583-1652), in the latter's *On the Ecclesiastical Hierarchy*. There Pétau argued that, while, in the primitive Church, the powers of the episcopate and presbyterate may sometimes have been conferred on the same individuals simultaneously, those powers remained, in principle, distinct throughout.[3] About the same time, another historian, the Oratorian Jean Morin (1591-1659), brought together liturgical evidence from both East and West to throw light on the nature of ordination.[4] He concluded that only two features of the ordination rite were of divine institution: the laying-on of hands and appropriate prayers, since these two were attested in Scripture and in the constant practice of the Church. Other ceremonies found in ordination rituals must simply be of ecclesiastical institution, though they might be considered, in the Church's practice, substantially requisite for validity in particular historical contingencies.[5]

Morin's work initiated a tremendous flurry of liturgiological activity. Among the delvers into the worship of the ancient Church, both Western and Eastern, the monks of the Congregation of St Maur, and the Dominican Jacques Goar (1601-1654) deserve special mention.[6] Perhaps this is a good point at which to note how vital liturgical evidence is in this connection. In the words of another Churchman of the period, Jacques-Bénigne Bossuet (1627-1704), the 'primary instrument of Tradition is enclosed in the prayers of the Church'.[7] As a modern student has written:

> The testimony of the liturgy is at once both objective and universal. There is no question here of special theory or the personal bias of a theologian, but of rites and prayers which are the authentic witness of the mind of the Church, since they were chosen by the Church herself to confer the sacrament of Order, entrusted to her by Christ. In the liturgy we are in direct contact with the living tradition of the Church — with the Church's own understanding of her ministry — the Church giving concrete expression to what theologians will later seek to convey in the technical language of sacrament, order and character. The ministries of episcopate, priesthood and diaconate were part of the life of the Church long before this technical vocabulary of sacramental theology was hammered out. To this living tradition the theologian must always return to find the reality underlying his theological concept.[8]

Not the least of the reasons why the theologian should thus constantly 'return' to the liturgical sources is to enable him to place his finger on those elements in Order which recur again and again: the constants in the Church's tradition. This is what Morin did in highlighting the central sacramental gesture from among the many lesser symbols with which the Church has surrounded it.

The eighteenth-century treatises on Order were able, at their best, to synthesise this treasury of liturgical material, along with other pertinent historical data, whilst preserving the dogmatic lines of reflection inherited from Trent, and from the high medievals who formed Trent's Scholastic background. In a typical work of the period, the author treats his subject as a diptych, its two wings devoted to the 'election' of candidates and their subsequent ordination. Thus, in François Hallier's *On Sacred Elections and Ordinations, in the Church's Use, Ancient and Modern,* 'elections' deal with a host of questions, moral, spiritual, pastoral and canonical, relevant to the choice of candidates for the sacrament of Order. Drawing on the Fathers' treatment of these issues, Hallier relates them carefully to the actual discipline proposed by the Council of Trent. By contrast, 'ordinations' is more strictly dogmatic, and deals with: the distinctness of orders; the existence of a sacrament of Order; the matter and form of the sacrament, with especial concern for the witness of the Eastern liturgies; the effects of the sacrament (character, and grace); the subject of ordination; its minister; the place and time of ordination, and its rites, which are accorded a lengthy symbolic commentary.[9]

Gradually, however, the wave of dogmatic treatises occasioned by the outbreak of the Reformation and the new improved historical methods of humanist scholarship, subsided into the earlier, medieval stream of writing about Order: the topic was absorbed, that is, into handbooks on theology at large, or, at best, treatises 'On the Sacraments'. We have reached, with the close of the eighteenth century, the era of the manuals. Yet the *spirituality* of the ordained ministry proved a topic of perennial interest. Throughout the period from Trent to the Catholic revival of the nineteenth century, and following the precedent set by the four patristic works already discussed, Order was approached from the viewpoint of what an increasingly departmentalised theological culture would call 'ascetical and mystical theology'. The authors of such works were exercised by how the ordained minister, and notably the presbyter, the priest, might grow in Christian virtue, and indeed in holiness, through his participation in the sacrament of Order.

This was not merely a literary task. Figures like Blessed John of Avila (1499-1569), St Philip Neri (1515-1595), St Cajetan and St Charles Borromeo (1480-1547) demonstrated a very practical zeal for the spiritual formation of the clergy. But 'the written word remains', and the characteristic teaching of such Catholic reforming figures was crystallised in such treatises as the Carthusian Anthony of Molina's (c.1590-1612) 'Instructions for Priests', with its sacramental and contemplative piety.[10] The historian of Order, Albert Michel, awarded its author the accolade 'doctor of the reform of clerics'.[11] Particularly influential, and long-lasting in its effects, was the so-called 'French School'.[12]

The single most important influence in the immediate background of the seventeenth century French School was the blueprint offered by François de la Rochefoucauld (1558-1645) in his *Estat ecclésiastique,* a work addressed to the clergy of the diocese of Clermont, and published at Lyons in 1597. In Rochefoucauld's vision, prayer was to be the ultimate source and constant vehicle of a sacerdotal spirituality, itself seen as the logical fulfilment of the ecclesiastical state. As Joseph Bergin, the reforming bishop's most recent biographer has written:

> It is ... significant that La Rochefoucauld devoted much of the *Estat* to the place of prayer in the life of the clergy, and to explaining its newest forms to them; he did so to such an extent that one commentator has written of him 'transforming his work into a treatise on prayer'. La Rochefocauld was eminently clear in his approach from the outset 'l'oraison est l'appuy principal de tout le reste des fonctions de cet estat' ['Prayer is the principal support of all the remaining functions of this estate']. The clergy should consider even the highest stages of interior prayer accessible to them — something earlier generations would have thought impossible. They might lack the advantages of the cloistered orders, but La Rochefoucauld insisted

that their activities should not be dismissed as so many distractions that made attentiveness to God impossible; they should, instead, turn regularly to God in prayer. This kind of prayer required a revolution within the clergy, and was possible only if they developed attitudes of penance, humility, and openness towards God. To La Rochefoucauld and, later, to the *école française,* the priest was pre-eminently a man of prayer, and therefore an acceptable mediator between God and men. The relationship between prayer and the ecclesiastical state was reciprocal. It oriented man towards God, but it was also the indispensable vehicle for the development of sacerdotal spirituality. It was not just one ecclesiastical activity among others: it was their essence.[13]

Against this significant background, Pierre de Bérulle (1575-1629), cardinal, founder of the Oratory of France, proposed that the ministerial priesthood should be seen, above all, in relation to the Incarnation.[14] The eternal Word had assumed humanity so that there might be a mediator between God and man. Through the humanity of Jesus Christ, the world gives glory to the Father, and the Father acts to transform the world, reconciling it to himself. Similarly, the ministerial priest is, in a double sense, a continuing mediator between God and man. For, on the one hand, he offers the worship of the faithful to the Father by uniting it with Christ's sacrifice through the Mass. And on the other hand, he acts as God's instrument in the transformation of the world, through evangelising and passing on divine teaching, especially in the context of the direction of souls, and by dispensing the mysteries of Christ's Body and Blood, and administering the other sacraments of the Church. (This twofold mediation may well remind us of Hippolytus' account of the bishop as high priest, representing the Church to God, and, as pastor, representing God to the Church.) Indebted as he was to Augustine's exemplarism, Bérulle sees Christ as the priest's archetype in the mystery of the Trinity, for the mission of the presbyter imitates the Father's sending forth of his Word.[15] The goal of God's plan, as of the priest's task, is the restoration of the bond between God and man which Bérulle, following sound etymology, sees as the heart of religion.

The central idea which animated Bérulle's Oratory may be stated as a simple proposition: the priesthood calls for perfection.[16] Although the validity of the sacraments in no way depends upon the holiness of their minister, the spiritual *rayonnement,* or 'shining forth', of the priest should always accompany his stewardship of the mysteries of God. Here Bérulle was helped by his reading of the Pseudo-Denys, for whose notion of hierarchy this was a commonplace. Bérulle found a confirmation of this thought in his own Christological emphasis: the self-emptying of the divine Son in the Incarnation and the Atonement, and notably in his self-gift to the disciples as their food in the anticipation of his sacrifice on Holy Thursday, in the Upper Room, gives the priest his marching orders. He, like Christ, is to be the victim of divine love, and, in serving, to reign. Thus Bérulle's emphasis on the interior life, the life of prayer, is not based on a general theory about the human spirit, but on the concrete demands of the following of Christ. For the Gospels show the Word Incarnate reciting a hymn with his own before imploring his Father in protracted prayer in the Garden of Olives. If each rank of the angels has its own devotion to some particular divine attribute (as the mystics of the Low Countries, whom Bérulle enjoyed reading, fancied), then the priest's special *attrait* can only be to the personal union of Godhead and manhood in Christ. On this the Abbé Michel Dupuy, the principal interpreter of Bérulle's doctrine of priesthood, has the following to say, drawing on the biblical notion of the apostolic minister as Christ's *shaliach,* 'representative', for guidance:

> If the priest is thus linked in a special way with the God-man, one can grasp what is defensible about this argument. It is true that meditation upon, and worship of, the hypostatic union must mark the spiritual life of the priest

even more than that of the lay-person, since the former shares more intimately in the priesthood of Christ which flows from that union. And for the priest to live his priesthood, it is not indispensable for him to question at length what it is he personally has received that the laity have not. It is far more important that he enter further into the God-man's mystery.[17]

Yet, the presbyter, unlike the monk, cannot be wholly occupied in contemplation. His is a public mission in the Church: his service to other human beings, and not simply his participation in the heavenly choir, renders him 'angelic'. The central act of this mission is the celebration of the Eucharist, wherein Christ extends his own incarnate existence, uniting himself not just to human *nature,* as at the Annunciation and at Christmas, but to each *person* who communicates. In the Mass, the priest is 'the conjoint instrument of the Son of God on earth'.[18] At the consecration, the divine Son draws the priest each day into the unity of his own person, joining him to his deified humanity, and making him, through the Eucharistic gifts, the dispenser of the Holy Spirit. This is why the priest, for his part, is to live only for Jesus, to subsist, by continual self-stripping, in Jesus, just as Jesus has no other personal existence than that of God the Word. The motive power of the priest's apostolate is the desire that the greatest possible number of people should offer, through their lives, the sacrifice of praise which the Eucharist brings to a climax. The idea of worship, then, unifies Bérulle's thought, and allows the apostolic perspective in his view of the ministry to remain, like the rest of his spiritual teaching, thorough-goingly theocentric.

Writers like St Vincent de Paul (1581-1660), the founder of the Congregation of the Mission (and the Daughters of Charity), Père Charles de Condren (1588-1641), Bérulle's successor as superior general of the Oratory, and Jean-Jacques Olier (1608-1657), founder of the Compagnie Saint-Sulpice, followed along the same lines.[19] These figures were related by close connections. Olier, for example, was the grateful recipient of the spiritual direction of, in turn, 'Monsieur Vincent' and de Condren. Condren's *L'Idée du sacerdoce et du sacrifice de Jésus Christ,* published in Paris in 1677, inspired Olier's *Traité des saints ordres* (IIIe partie). Most importantly, they exemplified in their lives the same high spiritual idea of the priesthood which they taught by the pen, or by word-of-mouth. That ideal has become part and parcel of the patrimony of Latin Catholicism: its fervour is well captured in de Condren's prayer for priests: *Jesu vivens in Maria.*

> Jesus that dost in Mary dwell,
> Be in thy servants' hearts as well,
> In the spirit of thy holiness,
> In the fulness of thy force and stress.
> In the very ways that thy life goes
> And virtues that thy pattern shows.
> In the sharing of thy mysteries;
> And every power in us that is
> Against thy power put under feet
> In the Holy Ghost the Paraclete
> To the glory of the Father. Amen.[20]

Although the Catholic reforms of the seventeenth century *milieu dévot* established associations of priests which seem comparable at first sight to religious orders, their aim was in fact to raise the educational, moral and spiritual level of the secular clergy by such methods as retreats and conferences, recognising as they did that the bishop's presbyterium has to carry the main burden of the apostolic ministry in the local church. When, through the instrumentality of, in particular, de Paul and Olier, the diocesan seminaries called for by the Council of Trent were established in France, it was this high doctrine of the priest, as the living extension of the ministry of the Word Incarnate, which they took as the star to steer by.

After the turbulence of the French Revolution — a purifying experience in that the destruction of the *ancien régime,* itself never fully permeable by the spirit of the Catholic Reform, led Churchmen to a more clear-sighted pursuit of the tenets and values of the faith, the French School produced its most illustrious priestly son in the person of St John Vianney, Curé d'Ars, Eventually to be declared patron of the secular clergy, he was held up as the model for all priests, whether secular or regular, by the Borromeo of the Second Vatican Council, Karol Wojtyla.[21]

Vianney prophesied, to Bishop William Bernard Ullathorne, the conversion of England to her ancient religious allegiance.[22] A number of the outstanding hierarchs who led the Catholic expansion of the later nineteenth century, produced tracts on the spirituality of the priesthood, which reproduced the biblical, patristic and Thomist qualities of French writing, but with the added touch of Anglo-Saxon concreteness and practicality. As an English Catholic, I will be forgiven my use of home-grown materials — which could be paralleled in, for example, Irish and American sources. Especially noteworthy in this respect was John Cuthbert Hedley (1837-1915), monk of Ampleforth and Bishop of Newport in the restored hierarchy,[23] though attention must also be given to the work of Henry Edward Manning (1808-1892), Oxford Movement convert and Archbishop of Westminster,[24] as to the emphasis on the priest as preacher of the Word found in the work of one who preceded him into Catholic communion, the Oratorian and cardinal, John Henry Newman (1801-1890).[25]

Hedley's *Lex Levitarum* is, in substantial part, a re-presentation of Gregory the Great's *Pastoral Rule* in contemporary dress.[26] Hedley was much concerned with helping the Church student towards his great goal. By 'vocation' and 'conversion', he wrote, 'this great aspiration may take shape and substance'. The sign of a priestly vocation is presented as natural inclination, together with the dispositions necessary for fulfilling what the priestly state of life requires or implies. As he tells his readers:

> One who holds in high esteem the state and duities of
> the priest, who feels himself drawn to them, who

experiences pleasure and satisfaction in the service of God, in a life of chastity, in prayer, in retirement and in sacred studies, and who is determined to seek in the pastoral office the honour of God alone and the salvation of his own soul and the souls of others — in him it is impossible to mistake the call of God.

And he advises the teachers and friends of such a person:

if we desire to have a proof of the genuineness of any one's inclinations towards the priesthood, and of the purity of his intention, there is none better than the earnest endeavour to cultivate the talents and powers given by God and to dispose and prepare oneself more and more for the due fulfilment of the pastoral office.[27]

Moving on from the continual conversion which authentic vocation will stimulate, Hedley explores the office of a pastor on the ground. Programmatically, the task of the pastor is

to administer and to apply those 'mysteries of God' which are in the world through the blood of the Cross.[28]

This involves consideration of the pastor's relation to his people as a flock, and as individuals. As a flock, he relates to them, in Hedley's view, in four ways. He gathers them together; he acts as a priest in their assemblies; he holds them in the unity of faith and obedience; and he walks with them as an example. But the people of God must also be treated as highly individual souls, each with a unique character, a distinctive set of requirements, virtues and failings. Relating himself to individuals, then, the pastor must be 'at the call of every sinner'; 'at the sickbed whenever death threatens'; and 'on the traces of every wandering and straying child of the heavenly Father'.[29]

But this concern for penitents, for the dying and the lapsed does not produce, at Hedley's hands, a gloomy picture of the priest's calling. He has a most positive account of the priest's necessary 'schooling of the heart'. The priest must learn how to turn physical and mental suffering into love. For Hedley, the priest's worst vices are ill temper and the 'habit of scolding' which, he warns, turn into querulousness, inconsiderateness and eventually childishness, by which the priest, as he agrees

> spoils the work of the Holy Spirit, and neutralises himself as one of the spiritual forces of the world.[30]

By contrast, the ordinand who grows in faithfulness to his vocation through continuing conversion, builds up what Gregory the Great had called the *soliditas timoris intimi,* or 'solid spiritual fear' which Hedley seeks to explain:

> certain views and certain ways of acting, learnt from spiritual sources, become firm, usual and habitual; the minds holds these views and principles as part of its equipment ... the will acts upon them promptly and easily, and the heart, on the whole, feels pleasure in carrying them out.[31]

These 'growths' of the heart and mind are based, Hedley tells us, on understanding of what Jesus Christ is to the world and the individual soul; on perception of the work of the Holy Spirit, and the need for the spiritualisation of the routine of life; on a recognition of the wisdom of the words and actions of the saints, and on some idea of the purifying and elevating force of suffering. Their symptoms are: regularity in prayer and the sacraments, greater mortification, more exact and diligent use of time in work, increase in loving union with God, Christ, our Lady and the saints, and an intelligent use of mental prayer.

Although Hedley's Benedictinism is apparent in his concern with the contemplative side of the priest's vocation, as also, as we shall see shortly, in his preoccupation with the continuing need for study, he is far from 'monasticising' the sacrament of Order. The pastor is distinguished from the contemplative, he argues, by an 'instinct of conquest'. The contemplative, like the pastor, hopes that he or she loves his neighbour's soul, but they do not have the same burning desire to encounter evils, to rescue souls, and to build up with its own exertions the visible Kingdom of God.[32]

Such 'devotedness', however, defeats itself if it loses touch with the life of prayer, because no one can persevere under the burden of the frequent failures that pastoral work involves unless he has a supernatural view of life and motive. Gregory the Great's own balance of inner and outer, contemplative and active, is apparent in the two virtues which Hedley highlights in a priest: *purity of heart* and *sympathy with souls*. The first, a 'purged spirit', includes

> the predominance of wisdom over impulse; the humility of the Catholic spirit, as contrasted with the seeking for novelties in faith; cleanness from carnal desires and from avarice; distinterestedness, as compared with self-seeking; and the absence of personal animus or envy or anger in dealing with others.[33]

'Sympathy with souls', entails what Hedley terms an 'impersonal', as contrasted with an 'abstract', self-identification with other people. This is a ready sympathy, aware of the distinctiveness of each person, and their peculiar needs, yet conscious also that

> The only thing that matters is that they are souls, to be helped and saved.[34]

We can too easily, Hedley maintains, approach the play of character in our human environment with the mind of a novelist, becoming absorbed in the aesthetic texture of the tragedy and comedy of human lives, and so forgetting the everlasting destiny of men and women.

More than half of *Lex Levitarum* is occupied with the role of study in the life of a priest, and whilst its author has in mind in the first place seminarians, he held that the habits of study formed in the seminary should continue to animate the work of the pastor. The years of 'philosophy and divinity' in the seminary are merely, for the student, the opening of his powers, and the beginning of serious intellectual work.[35]

The ordained man who neglects to follow this up is submitted by Hedley to a substantial drop of acid from the pen. He will be, in all probability:

> a poor creature to the end of his career, incapable of sustained thought, never ready with an idea or a fact, looking upon scientific theology as a pedantic accomplishment instead of seeing that it is an education, professing to admire the Penny Catechism, which he is quite unable to comment upon, lauding common sense, which with him really means narrowness and laziness, utterly unskilled in that development of an idea, or that telling arrangement of matter, without which a sermon is a tissue of crudeness and of incoherence, spending his leisure, and more than he has a right to call his leisure, in newspapers and light reading.[36]

To move from Hedley's work to that of Manning is to pass on to a writer equally concerned with the moral and spiritual dimensions of the priesthood, but more anxious to place these within a dogmatic framework. *The Eternal Priesthood* was written out of the conviction that the growth in holiness of the presbyterate should be a major preoccupation of the bishop.[37] Its main thesis is that the ministerial priesthood is, in and of itself, an outstanding way to perfection, and even a 'state of perfection' — a life whose duties are such that their worthy performance is enough to perfect the Christian discipleship of the person living it, and to bring him to sanctity. Manning justified these assertions by a pneumatological reading of the doctrine of sacramental character, as found in St Thomas. Manning was especially interested in the study of the economy of the Holy Spirit, whom he evidently considered a somewhat neglected divine Person, as his books on the outer mission and inner working of the Holy Spirit bear witness. Here he provided an original interpretation of Thomas in the light of this predominantly pneumatological approach to dogma, with interesting results.

According to Manning, when St Thomas remarks that the priestly character is conferred not on the essence of the soul but on its powers, he has in mind something that happens to the intellect 'by way of light' and to the affections, 'by way of love'. But light and love, as the New Testament and the liturgical tradition alike bear witness, are the tell-tale signs of the work of the Holy Spirit. The character signifies then, in Manning's words:

> a work of the Holy Ghost the Illuminator and Sanctifier upon the soul. But it signifies not only the universal and uniform work of the Holy Ghost, as in Baptism and Confirmation, but a special and singular work wrought upon the soul of those only who by Ordination share in the priesthood of Jesus Christ.[38]

Moreover, appealing once more to Thomas, the sacramental character is the 'formal cause' of sacramental grace: that is, it makes that grace the *kind* of grace it is. Just as, in Baptism the character of child of God conferred by that sacrament contains all the grace needed for the life of such a child, and as in Confirmation, similarly, the character has within it all the grace needed 'for the warfare of the soldiers of Jesus Christ, even to confessorship and martyrdom', so here also:

> the character of priesthood has in it all graces of light, strength and sanctity needed for the sacerdotal life in all its manifold duties, trials and dangers.[39]

And Manning refers in this connection to Paul's advice to Timothy (1 Tm 4:14) not to neglect the grace given him through the imposition of hands. In encouraging the ministerial priest to find, in his distinctive sacrament, a certain light and warmth for the spirit, Manning, without being aware of the fact, re-created the doctrine of Thomas' Franciscan contemporary Bonaventure on the sacramental character.[40]

Manning's account of the roles of the priesthood, taking its

cue from that of Thomas, considers the presbyter as bearer of
a twofold power: *vis-à-vis* Christ's *Eucharistic* and his *mystical*
body. On the first, Manning is positively Bérullian in his claim
that the anaphora of the Mass continue the Incarnation and
Oblation of the divine Son. On the second, he shows himself
anxious to preserve as many biblical titles and images for the
apostolic minister as possible. The latter is at once steward,
ambassador, judge, physician, but above all — for Manning
— *father,* referring to Paul's claims to spiritual parenthood in
1 Corinthians 4:15. (This explains Manning's campaign to give
the secular clergy, a phrase he disliked anyway, the title 'Father',
like their regular counterparts.) He stresses, in a native English
version of the *école française,* the priest's call to perfect
discipleship.

> It is ..... always to be borne in mind that a priest is ordained
> *ad exercendam perfectionem* — that is, not only to be perfect,
> but by his own life, and by the action and influence of
> his life in word and deed on others, to exhibit and to
> impress on them the perfection of our divine Lord.[41]

In this, the priest is helped not only by the sacramental grace
of his priesthood, but also by the exercise of its sacred duties,
and notably of the pastoral office, which Manning presents as
a life of self-abnegation since it is a discipline of charity: a Cross
and Resurrection in miniature. To these 'general instrumental
means of perfection', Manning adds an entire inventory of
'special' means also; ranging from the law of celibacy and the
spirit of poverty, through obedience to the Church, a habit
of prayer, daily Mass and visits with the divine Friend in the
Tabernacle, to suggestions more characteristically his own.
Among these latter, worth singling out are Manning's subtle
account of the moral insights to be gained from the hearing
of confessions; his stress on preaching the Word of God —
suitably prepared by the study of the Bible — as itself a way
of ministerial holiness, and, finally, what he terms the 'law of
liberty'. Pointing out that, since the priest, unlike most lay
Christians, has enormous freedom in the disposition of his own

time, Manning regards him as particularly well suited to embody the gracious — that is, grace-filled — living characteristic of the Gospel.

> In Jesus Christ we see a will that is a law to itself; and all who are like him in the measure of their likeness become their own law in the use of their liberty. This law leaves behind it all literal commandments, as the learned become unconscious of the alphabet, and the skilful singer unconscious of the score. It is a law more constraining than any commandment ....[42]

Manning's account of the priest's life ranges from the prose of suggestions about a sensible time-plan for the day, and ways of decorating one's house, to the poetry of an almost mystical exploration of priestly consciousness at its highest. The priest's 'rewards' lie not only in the joy of a pastor over his flock and in that end which was never far from Manning's own thoughts, a happy death, but in a way of enjoying both nature and grace to which the 'law of liberty' gives the key.

> A priest who has nothing but his bare subsistence enjoys without burden or responsibility all the works of nature in all their brightness and sweetness, and that in a higher degree, perhaps, than the lord of the soil. The beauty of the world is a common inheritance, and none enjoy it so keenly as those who by the *donum scientiae* see God in everything and everything in God. The whole world to them is like the bush that burned on Mount Horeb.[43]

And again:

> 'All things are theirs'; and this includes the whole revelation of God, and the whole regeneration of mankind ... A priest whose mind is filled with the eternal world will be always — habitually and virtually, and very often actually — filled with its light, peace and gladness.[44]

Manning's concern with priestly holiness, then, like that of Hedley, constitutes an English version of the post-Tridentine ideal of priesthood worked out in France. It will be echoed by the decree *Presbyterorum ordinis* of the Second Vatican Council. For that document set out to offer not only a theology of the ministerial priesthood but a blueprint for the existence of the ministerial priest, for his life-story. It was, as its full title claimed, an account of the 'life and ministry of priests'.

Before turning, however, to the twentieth-century theology of Order which forms the more immediate background to the Council's teaching, we should pause to consider the significant stress — *significant,* since a sign or pointer to the work of that Council — placed on the priest's ministry of the Word in the third of our Victorian triumvirate, John Henry Newman.

Newman's emphasis on preaching as the first duty of bishops, both as Anglican and as Catholic, with its necessary implications for both presbyters and deacons in their functions as 'guardians of the preaching bishop' was, in G.W. Rutler's words, 'possibly unsurpassed by any Christian writing' in the period before the Second Vatican Council.[45]

> He did take with him to Rome an uncommon reverence for the preaching of Scripture. In language which would be repeated at Vatican Two, he said that Scripture had the 'nature' though not the 'sacredness' of a sacrament. Moreover, in his *Grammar* he proceeded to define Christianity as 'an announcement, a preaching'. He marvelled that his fellow Catholics had so much lost the ancient perspective of the two tables well represented by Saint Augustine who had identified 'our daily bread' sacramentally with both the Word of God and the Eucharist.[46]

If Newman's original awareness of this Augustinian perspective was mediated by John Wesley, who had taken it from the late medieval devotional classic *The Imitation of Christ,* as a Catholic Newman came to see it embodied in spectacular fashion in the person of St Philip Neri, and his Roman Oratory which

Newman himself proposed to re-create for the people of Birmingham.[47] To preach the Gospel in a society whose world view had changed perhaps more radically than that of any other age, demanded, in Newman's view, the energetic and imaginative exploitation of the preacher's task and gifts.

> The prophetic preacher proclaims the Gospel not as an imposition of the teaching of Christ but as representation of Christ the Teacher; the priestly preacher ministers the Word as a mediation and sacrifice by which the hearers may be sanctified by Christ the High Priest; the kingly preacher initiates and completes the process as builder and shepherd of the community of faith by declaring the elemental facts of redemption and guarding that *kerygma* with the authority commissioned by Christ the King. Newman's exposition of these offices, sometimes oblique and sometimes systematic, was a preview of the three ways in which the Council described the renewal of the priesthood.[48]

It is to that crucial idea of the mid-twentieth-century theology of priesthood, the threefold office, and to the Council's fresh synthesis of ancient elements, that we must now turn.

From the Catholic Revival to the Second Vatican Council

In terms of the twentieth-century theology of priesthood which links in time the masters of the Catholic Revival to the Second Vatican Council, the French School's notion of the priest as continuator of the Word Incarnate retained a powerful subterranean influence. For in the Catholic theology of the first fifty years of the twentieth century, the sacrament of Order is seen as a sacrament which re-presents, *represents* in the strongest possible sense of that term, the unique ministry of Jesus Christ himself.[1] Office in the Church, according to a wide variety of writers in all the main European languages, is a representation of the offices of Christ himself, the main differentiations of his mission as the Messiah. If the primordial sacrament of God is the humanity of Jesus, whereby the divine life becomes accessible to us in a human way, how is its saving work perpetuated after the Ascension? Is there a visible continuation of the activity of the Word Incarnate? By answering that question in terms of the Church and its office-holders, Catholic theologians found themselves gravitating naturally to an account of Order as the re-presentation of the offices of Christ.[2]

For some, it sufficed to speak of a twofold office, whether of Christ or of the Church and so of its office-holders. The Swiss ecclesiologist Cardinal Charles Journet, for example, dealt with the matter in terms of, on the one hand, the priestly *munus* exercised by Christ, and by the apostolic hierarchy in dependence on Christ, and, on the other, of the royal or pastoral *munus,* which he regarded as including the prophetic or teaching office within itself.[3] To call humanity to a condition of obedience to God, as its rightful king or shepherd, is inevitably to teach people as prophet what it is they should believe (faith) and what it is they should do (morals). The advantage of treating the work of the Word Incarnate, and so the sacrament of his ordained ministers in terms of such a *munus duplex* was, among other things, that it enabled theologians to recuperate what their medieval and Tridentine predecessors had to say about the two 'powers' of the apostolic ministry: the *potestas ordinis,* concerned with celebrating the Eucharist and the other sacraments, which Journet and his fellows linked to the priestly office properly so called, and the *potestas jurisdictionis,* concerned with governing the People of God, and therefore with teaching them, which formed the foundation of pastoral care and doctrinal mission.[4] So far as the ordained were concerned, the twofold office was frequently described as giving those who represented Christ the Priest and King power over, first, his Eucharistic body, and secondly, his mystical body. In a somewhat crude form, this theology of Order perceived that the common factor in the tasks of the ordained is the body of Christ, a body at once Eucharistic and ecclesial.

However, more important for the future was the theology which spoke of the ordained as representing the *munus triplex,* or *three*fold office, of Christ. First of all, a word about where it came from. Although there are hints of this kind of Christological scheme in the patristic period, its systematic use is a Reformation development. It appears to have entered the mainstream of Catholic theology in two ways. The main channel was German-speaking Catholic theologians who borrowed it from their Lutheran counterparts in the course of the eighteenth century. The other vehicle of this type of Christological analysis was John Henry Newman, who himself seems to have taken it from Calvin's *Institutes.* Newman had applied it not only to the Church at large but, quite explicitly, to her ministry in particular.[5] From the beginning of the twentieth century onwards, this threefold analysis of the representative task of the Church *vis-à-vis* the work of Christ grew in popularity until it finally swept the board by being incorporated into the two main ecclesiological encyclicals of Pope Pius XII: *Mystici Corporis Christi* of 1943 and *Mediator Dei* of 1947. It was from these encyclicals that it passed into the texts of the Second Vatican Council.

The theological decision to present both episcopate and presbyterate in terms of a share in Christ's threefold office has advantages and disadvantages. Its advantages are, first, a Christocentricity which refuses to speak about the work of the ordained ministry except in terms of the work of Jesus Christ of which it is a sacramental continuation, and secondly, the possibilities it creates for clear exposition, given its tidy demarcation of the tasks of the ordained ministry into cultus, teaching and pastoral government. Its disadvantages are mainly a matter of the inconveniences which can arise, if not guarded against, from that very tidiness. For there is a danger that, following this schema, we may keep separate things that are in fact connected. For instance, the teaching office of the bishops or the teaching mandate of the presbyter, are not things wholly separate from their pastoral functions in the Church. On the contrary, the pastoral office gives the teaching office its proper modality. Thus, while bishops and priests are under no obligation to become theologians (though it helps if they do!), they are to teach the faith in such a way that the people committed to their charge live ever more deeply with the mind of the Son and the life of the Spirit. As this example suggests, the way in which the bishop and presbyter participate in the office of prophet cannot be separated from their share in the office of shepherd. Nor can the office of priest be left out of the picture in describing the proper mode of the teaching that goes on thanks to the prophetic office, which is a teaching that leads Christ's faithful to the adoration of the Father 'in the Spirit and in truth'. So the three offices as found in each order are ultimately triune, three-in-one, just as is the sacrament of Order itself, displayed in its three 'grades'.

Second, analysing the task of the ordained ministry into a set of offices also produces the temptation to make the trio of offices an order of priorities. Thus for instance, someone might wish to play down the cultic or liturgical work of a presbyter on the grounds that it was very secondary when compared with proclamation, preaching and teaching. Or again, some other party might wish, perhaps in reaction against just such playing down, to set in motion the reverse process, once more with unfortunate results. For in these ways, we may, if we are careless, rend into pieces the seamless garment of the apostolic ministry. With whatever variations, there is a pattern to the ordained ministry, not least in its two priestly forms, those of the bishop and the presbyter. The ministerial task has an overall unity, made up of a number of elements which fructify each other. What these may be we must briefly consider before this book ends. The story of the sacrament of Order itself tells us what they are.

By the time the Second Vatican Council opened, the development of Catholic theology, ratified by some important acts of the papal magisterium, had made possible, for the first time in the Church's history, a full doctrinal account of the sacrament of Order. Two features of the teaching of Pope Pius XII, not yet mentioned, should be noticed. One of these was Pius' letter *Sacramentum Ordinis* of 1948 in which, fortified by historical scholarship, the Pope ruled that the crucial sacramental gesture of Order, its 'matter', was the laying-on of hands — and not any of the alternatives features of the ordination rite suggested by earlier theologians.[6] Again, in *Mediator Dei* of the previous year — an encyclical about the Liturgy and so necessarily also a document about the priestly office of bishop and presbyter — Pope Pius stressed that the distinctive feature of the ministerial priesthood, as against that of the universal priesthood, was that it represented Christ the Head, *vis-à-vis* his own body, his Church-body, the Christian laity.[7]

So far as other issues raised by the story of this sacrament were concerned, the opening of the Council found Catholic thought in a remarkably settled state. As regards the diaconate — which, the reader may have noticed, has disappeared from our story with the close of the Middle Ages — there was general agreement that it had fallen on hard times, and needed some form of reinvigoration and reinstatement. Where the presbyterate was concerned, the thesis that it consisted of a participation in the fullness of the ministerial priesthood enjoyed by the bishop could command widespread support. Only a few Thomists opposed it. Admittedly, despite Manning and company, not everyone accepted the claim that the ministerial priesthood was in itself a state of perfection. But the only really major issue left unresolved by the history of what may be termed the technical theology of Order concerned the episcopate, and, more precisely, the origins of episcopal jurisdiction. By this was meant not so much the historical origins of the episcopal office of governance in the apostolic Church but rather the manner in which, today, a bishop receives his authority to share in the ruling of the universal Church.[8] The division lay between 'immediatists' and 'mediatists'. Both sides agreed that episcopal jurisdiction in one sense derives immediately from God. They agreed that by divine institution there will always be bishops in the Church, governing the faithful in due hierarchical communion with the Roman pontiff. The dispute between them concerned the manner in which such episcopal jurisdiction was received by an individual bishop. Immediatists claimed that it was conferred immediately, without anyone else's mediation, at the bishop's consecration. For them, the canonical institution of a bishop by the pope merely limited this jurisdiction to a determinate portion of the faithful. It did not confer it. For mediatists, on the other hand, although episcopal jurisdiction derives from Christ as its first cause or source, it is mediated by the pope when he institutes other bishops as pastors of the Church, or when, as with Oriental bishops, he tacitly acknowledges their institution by other means. This debate lies behind the relevant section of *Lumen Gentium* (21–22) on the office of bishop, and has its importance, since it concerns the character of Peter's relations with the Twelve, singly or together, in that sacramental continuation of the original apostolic college which is the episcopate with, and under, its papal head.

At the same time, the development of a theology of the laity, in which the contribution of the Dominican Yves Congar was crucial, invited theologians to situate the apostolic ministry, in its threefold differentiation, in terms of the 'universal and royal priesthood' of the Christian people as such. They rose to the challenge: a typical voice might be that of the *Spiritain* Père Joseph Lécuyer in his masterpiece, *Le Sacerdoce dans le Mystère du Christ*. There Lécuyer proposes that the ministerial priesthood in its two degrees, presbyteral and episcopal, constitutes the sacrament, in the Church, of the priesthood of Christ as Head of the mystical body. In the Eucharist and Penance, proper to the presbyter (and to the bishop who is also *sumpresbyteros*, a co-presbyter with his brethren), Christ's Easter victory is applied to human beings, as a new life to God which means, of necessity, the destruction of an old life sunk in sin. In Confirmation and the transmission of Order itself, proper to the bishop, Christ's sending forth, from the Father, of the Pentecostal Spirit equips the people of God, the laity with their clergy, for its mission in the world. But Lécuyer admonishes:

> One will remember that the hierarchical priesthood, which represents the priesthood of the Head of the mystical body and is its sacrament in the sense that we have just explained, so far from excluding the priesthood of all the members of that mystical body, constantly presupposes that priesthood. The hierarchical priesthood is established for the functioning of the whole body which is the Church, and for the good of that body, so that all its members may actualise the spiritual sacrifice which gives them access, with Jesus, to the true sanctuary. It is, then, in union with all the baptised that the hierarchical priesthood offers the sacrifice of the Paschal mystery, and, with the collaboration of all the confirmed that, in the New Covenant, it realises the apostolic mission of the new People of God.[9]

The Second Vatican Council

It is time to turn to the documents of the Council itself. The Council devoted two documents exclusively to Order, one to bishops, *Christus Dominus,* and one to priests, *Presbyterorum ordinis,* the latter having as a pendant the decree on priestly formation, *Optatam totius.* These texts focus on the pastoral responsibilities of bishops and priests, and so are as much ascetical or moral in tone as they are doctrinal. The main dogmatic-theological investment of the Council on this subject is found in *Lumen gentium,* its dogmatic constitution on the Church.

Fundamentally, what *Lumen gentium* has to say about Order concerns the episcopate, and only a small section deals with the presbyterate and diaconate. In a strongly worded statement, the Council affirms the divine origin of the episcopate:

> This sacred Synod teaches that by divine institution bishops have succeeded to the place of the apostles as shepherds of the Church...so that he who hears them, hears Christ.[10]

In this statement, the Council resolved a disagreement in Catholic theology reaching back to the fourth century and deliberately left open by Trent: an interesting example of Vatican II being *more* willing to define doctrine than its Tridentine predecessor. By their consecration, the bishops receive the fullness of the sacrament of Order, a fullness which the text describes in terms of a threefold *munus* — sanctifying, teaching and governing, corresponding to Christ's own threefold office as Priest, Prophet and King. *Lumen gentium* also describes the ultimate purpose of this threefold episcopal office in the Church. It explains that, so as to provide for the continuance of his mission, Christ formed his apostles into a fixed group or college, over which he placed Peter. The members of this college he sent out

> so that as sharers in his power they might make all peoples his disciples.[11]

Thus the point of the episcopate, and so of the ministerial priesthood of which the episcopate is the fullness, lies in bringing this world to an effective acknowledgement of the reign of Christ. It coheres with this that the Council arranges the threefold office of the bishops in a sequence of teaching, sanctifying, pastorate. Assuming that this order is not accidental, and that it is not to be interpreted chronologically, as the order of what happens when a local church is created, then it would signify that the bishops are primarily teachers or evangelists; secondly, stewards of the Church's worship, and thirdly, pastors or governors of their particular churches. We recall that, historically, it is because the bishop has inherited from the apostles (or 'apostolic men') the duty of guarding the deposit, and of ordaining others to be stewards of the mystery of worship, that he, the head of the local presbyterium of pastors, is to his own church what the apostles were to the Church universal.

What *Lumen Gentium* has to say about, on the one hand, the offices conferred by episcopal consecration and, on the other, the exercise of those offices, throws light on how the bishops are related to the pope — typologically, the Twelve to Peter — as well as resolving a dispute at least as old as Trent. As the Dogmatic Constitution insists, these offices are to be exercised 'in hierarchical communion with the head and members of the body' (of the apostles' successors).[12] An explanatory note added by the Council's Doctrinal Commission spelt out what this means.[13] Consecration brings immediately with it all three *munera,* including that of pastoral rule. Yet the empowerment to act directly in the exercise of this rule (as of the other offices) requires additionally the intervention (explicit or no) of the head of the episcopal college. This follows from the very nature of the sacrament of Order: even, or rather *especially* in those who receive it in its fullness (the bishops), it implies hierarchical communion — and so some reference to the special prerogatives of the pope. As Père Jean Galot has pointed out, the two 'powers', order and jurisdiction, identified by the medievals are not really two distinct realities at all. Instead, there is a single power, *exousia,* of the sacrament of Order, along with a concrete enactment as to the domain in which this power will be exercised.[14]

Turning to the other sacred Orders: *Lumen gentium* goes on

to speak of the bishops, in their capacity as the apostles' successors:

> legitimately handing on to different individuals in the Church various degrees of participation in (their) ministry.[15]

This it sees as the origin of the presbyterate and diaconate — at least when considered in the formal perspective of dogmatic theology. The Council, however, regards the presbyterate and diaconate as very different sorts of participation in the episcopal ministry. Using a distinction found in the early third century *Egyptian Church Order,* it sees deacons as ordained not for priesthood but for a 'ministry of service'.[16] Presbyters, on the other hand, are ordained to so considerable a share in the apostolic ministry of the bishop that they can rightly be called *sacerdotes,* 'priests'.[17] They image Christ the eternal Priest by participating in his unique mediatorship between God and the world. The threefold office of Christ, as reflected in the bishop's functions, is also mirrored in that of the presbyter, who is the teacher, shepherd and sanctifier of that portion of God's flock entrusted to him. Here we see once again the characteristic post-Nicene presbyter, the mini-bishop in his parish. For the deacon, on the other hand, this typology does not hold good. He serves the people of God by a threefold ministry of worship, teaching and charity, but this reproduces the triple *munus* of Christ only imperfectly. Most notably, the deacon is not a pastor or shepherd. He has no sacramentally bestowed authority to lead or govern. The empty space left by this absence of a pastoral ministry is occupied in his case by the works of charity — typically, by administering the Church's goods in the interests of the poor. However, even if the Council strongly implies that the deacon is in no sense a ministerial priest, unlike the bishop and presbyter, it does assert that his office is fully sacramental in character. The single sacrament of Order, then, exists in three modes — episcopal, presbyteral and diaconal — of which only two can be called priestly. This teaching by the Council disqualifies the theological opinion, occasionally met with, which regards the deacon as someone co-opted by sacramentally ordained ministers to help in realising the aims of Order, but not as being himself a sacramental person. For further enlightenment as to how contemporary Church authority sees the diaconate, one should consult Pope Paul VI's decrees *Sacrum diaconatus ordinem* of June 1967, and *Ad pascendum* of August 1972. These put into operation the Council's call for a restoration of the permanent diaconate, not least for married men. This was the fruit of a movement which had begun in the Germany of the 1930s: married deacons, engaged in secular occupations could, it was hoped, make a significant contribution to catechesis, liturgy and preaching.[18] Paul VI's documents, in conformity to tradition, define the deacon's place in the local church in terms of his reference not to a parish priest but to the bishop. In practice, however, the deacon is in most cases a minister assistant to a presbyter encharged with a parish, a situation which reflects the character of a *parochus* throughout the history of the parochial system. He is, as we have seen, a scaled down version of the bishop in a miniature version of the local church.

The Council's teaching on the presbyterate, both in *Lumen gentium* and in *Presbyterorum ordinis,* shows two theological tendencies which deserve comment. First, in opposing a long-standing danger of reducing the theological significance of the episcopate in favour both of the Petrine office-holder and of the presbyterate, the Council was in some danger of going to the opposite extreme, at least where the presbyterate was concerned. (Paul VI, as is well-known, intervened in the debate over the bishops, to prevent the subordination of the Papacy to the episcopate, and so the loss of a freedom of action hard won in the course of the nineteenth century.) The conciliar texts, by stressing that the presbyter receives his sacrament by receiving a share in that of the bishop, and acts not only as the bishop's assistant, but also as his vicar, surrogate and extension, can give the impression that the only reason for having a presbyterate in the Church is that the bishops cannot do everything themselves. But as we have seen from investigating the New Testament and early patristic evidence, the presbyterate is by no means so thoroughly derivative from the episcopate, and parasitic upon it, as this might suggest. The presbyterate is the original ordained ministry of the local church. Although the significance of the presbyterate was naturally affected when chief presbyters with *episkopê* inherited the universal, rather than local, ministry of the apostles, the emergence of the episcopate as *the* apostolic ministry *par excellence* cannot overthrow the fact that the presbyterate is itself an apostolic creation. Moreover, as one contemporary scholar has written:

> Though...the presbyterate took on various forms and was viewed in various ways, the liturgical and patristic evidence....shows the prevailing conviction that the order of presbyters has always belonged to that providential disposition whereby God has determined the composition of the Church's hierarchy. The paradigms of the sons of Aaron and the elders of Israel, as well as the *secundi praedicatores* or the seventy-two disciples as types or figures of the presbyters of the Church, are evidence of this.[19]

Here, as everywhere, the Council's texts, just because they are texts, need interpreting, and the proper context for their interpretation, as with the work of any Council, is that of Tradition as a whole.

The presbyterate, then, is not something unfolded from out of the episcopate. It is an order existing alongside the episcopate, and in its own right. The Council texts implicitly acknowledge this when they exhort the bishops to consult their presbyteries in decision-making, to treat presbyters as their friends and brothers, and to establish senates of priests to assist them in the governing of their particular churches. The bishop's duty to do such things would be theologically inexplicable if the presbyterate were simply the creation of the episcopate — a kind of extension of the bishop's person. Such forms of episcopal-presbyteral co-operation introduce a note of collegiality into the pastoral ministry of the local church, so that this characteristic of the ministry is not found only on the universal level of the ministry of bishops.[20]

Yet, taken in its entirety, *Presbyterorum ordinis* is a very thorough and comprehensive piece of work. It does not bear out the claim sometimes made that the Council neglected to give serious consideration to the priesthood as such. The text may be regarded as a synthesis of the materials we have been looking at in the course of this study. It shows the signs of all the main periods which have contributed to the development of the Catholic understanding of the priesthood: from the New Testament, through the Fathers to the medievals; from Trent, through the successive attempts to realise the Tridentine ideal, to the insights of the dogmatic theologians of the first half of this century. *Presbyterorum ordinis* is a palimpsest, in which all these hands can be discerned at different points. So much is clear from the *references* appended to the document, which range from Scripture, the Fathers and St Thomas to Trent and the modern popes, not forgetting the evidence of the Liturgy and its formulations. But more importantly, it is a matter of the *themes* which the Council fathers felt ought to be treated. Thus, looking to the New Testament foundations, *Presbyterorum ordinis* considers the priesthood, firstly, in the light of the apostolic ministry given by Christ to his disciples.

> Since they share in the function of the apostles in their own degree, priests are given the grace by God to be the ministers of Jesus Christ among the nations, fulfilling the sacred task of the Gospel, that the oblation of the gentiles may be made acceptable and sanctified in the Holy Spirit.[21]

Secondly, it lists the kinds of activity which make up the special role of the presbyterate in the Church, rather as did the patristic ordination prayers. These it groups under three heads: priests as ministers of God's Word; as ministers of the sacraments, and especially of the Eucharist; as rulers of God's people. Some words illustrative of each may be in place:

> It is the first task of priests as co-workers of the bishops to preach the Gospel of God to all men... Priests...owe it everybody to share with them the truth of the Gospel in which they rejoice in the Lord.[22]

> The purpose...for which priests are consecrated by God through the ministry of the bishop is that they should be made sharers in a special way in Christ's priesthood and, by carrying out sacred functions, act as his ministers who through his Spirit continually exercises his priestly function for our benefit in the liturgy.[23]

> In the name of the bishop they gather the family of God as a brotherhood endowed with the spirit of unity and lead it in Christ through the Spirit to God the Father.[24]

Thirdly, *Presbyterorum ordinis* reinforces the idea of the sacramental character of the ordained worked out by medieval theology. Through the sacrament of Order

> priests by the anointing of the Holy Spirit are configured to Christ the Priest in such a way that they are able to act in the person of Christ the Head.[25]

Fourthly, the text treats the priesthood in the closest connection with the Eucharist, as had the Council of Trent before it. Indeed, it states frankly, speaking of the Eucharistic sacrifice:

> the ministry of priests is directed to this and finds its consummation in it.

That ministry, though commencing in the proclamation of the Gospel, draws all its power from Christ's sacrifice as offered

> through the priests' hands in the name of the whole Church in an unbloody and sacramental manner until the Lord himself come.[26]

And where the notion of the centrality of the Eucharist is

concerned, a more forthright statement than the following could hardly be imagined:

> The other sacraments, and indeed all ecclesiastical ministries and works of the apostolate, are bound up with the Eucharist and are directed towards it. For in the most blessed Eucharist is contained the whole spiritual good of the Church, namely Christ himself our Pasch and the living Bread who gives life to men through his flesh — that flesh which is given life and gives life through the Holy Spirit. Thus men are invited and led to offer themselves, their works and all creation with Christ. For this reason the Eucharist appears as the source and the summit of all preaching of the Gospel: catechumens are gradually led up to participation in the Eucharist, while the faithful who have already been incorporated in baptism and confirmation are fully incorporated in the Body of Christ by the reception of the Eucharist. Therefore the eucharistic celebration is the centre of the assembly of the faithful over which the priest presides.[27]

Fifthly, *Presbyterorum ordinis* is concerned with the personal holiness of the priest, like the French School, and suggests concrete ways whereby the members of the presbyterate may grow in holiness, as had the writers of the nineteenth-century English Catholic revival. Thus, it declares that, whilst all Christians have received a call to perfection,

> priests are bound by a special reason to acquire this perfection. They are consecrated to God in a new way in their ordination and are made the living instruments of Christ the eternal Priest, and so are enabled to accomplish throughout all time that wonderful work of his which with supernatural efficacy restores the whole human race.

And the text continues:

Since every priest in his own way assumes the person of Christ he is endowed with a special grace. By this grace the priest, through his service of the people committed to his care and all the People of God, is able the better to pursue the perfection of Christ whose place he takes. The human weakness of his flesh is remedied by the holiness of him who became for us a High Priest 'holy, innocent, undefiled, separated from sinners'.[28]

Among the means to holiness, the Council text places first and foremost the demands of the threefold presbyteral office itself, since that office not only requires holiness but actually fosters it. Familiarity with the Word of God in the prophetic office; identification with Christ as priest and victim in the daily offering of the Eucharistic Sacrifice, and union with Christ's charity through the administration of the other sacraments, as by the intercessory work of the divine Office, in the priestly office; the seeking what will benefit the many, rather than one's own convenience, in the pastoral office — the decree can find no aids to presbyteral holiness to mention before these. In conformity, however, with the spiritual tradition inherited from, above all, the Church of the seventeenth century, *Presbyterorum ordinis* goes on to cite as 'helps toward fostering the interior life' of priests: the fruitful reception of the sacrament of Penance; daily examination of conscience; devotion to Mary as 'protectress of their ministry'; 'visiting' Jesus Christ in the *Sanctissimum,* the sacrament of the altar; retreats and spiritual direction; and, not least, *oraison.*

In various ways, in particular through the approved practice of mental prayer and the different forms of vocal prayer which they freely choose to practice, priests are to seek and perseveringly ask of God the true spirit of adoration. By this spirit, they themselves, and with them the people entrusted to their care, will unite themselves with Christ the Mediator of the New Testament, and will be able as adopted sons to cry, 'Abba, Father'.[29]

Sixthly, the authors of the decree accept, as already stated, the fundamental Christological typology of the threefold office, as worked out by the early twentieth-century theology of Order:

> Through the sacred ordination and mission which they receive from the bishops, priests are promoted to the service of Christ the Teacher, Priest and King.[30]

The text, moreover, makes its own the view of Pope Pius XII that these three offices, in the case of the ordained, as distinct from that of the laity, are exercised specifically in the name of Christ as *Head* of his mystical body.[31]

Presbyterorum ordinis emerges, therefore, as a fine synthesis of the distinctive insights contributed by the principal stages which the theology of the sacrament of Order has undergone.[32] It remains, in conclusion, to collate its materials in the shape of a portrait of the presbyter, that central figure in the triptych of bishop, priest and deacon in the apostolic ministry of the Church.

Conclusion

A major source of the crisis of the priesthood in the post-conciliar period lies in the fact that people lost a sense for the complex unity of the priestly life, so that when they heard the word 'priest', no coherent image was suggested by it.[1] The presbyterate, overwhelmingly the most numerous membership of the 'brotherhood of holy pastors', and the 'order' which carries, to a marked degree, the burden of the everyday work of the apostolic ministry, lives by a *pattern* composed of a variety of elements.[2] It is not correct to dissolve this pattern by reducing its elements simply to those which can only be carried out by a priest: namely the consecration of the Eucharistic elements and the absolution of penitents. The pattern, which is the fruit of two thousand years of the development of both doctrine and practice, must be cherished and nurtured for itself. Its elements are, so far as I can see, nine in number. They are:

1. evangelising the unconverted;
2. teaching sound doctrine in faith and morals to the converted;
3. forming others to be apostolic;
4. celebrating the sacraments, and other rites of the Church;
5. in particular, by the celebration of Penance and the Eucharist, bringing the Paschal Mystery to bear on the lives of the faithful, who die to sin, and live with Christ to God;
6. in the Mass, but also in the divine Office, acting as intercessor for the Church, and for all creation;
7. in union with the bishop, and, ultimately, with the pope, to build up, as pastor, the communion of the Church, gathering the faithful and opening them to the fullness of the Church's life;
8. visiting, and so counselling and encouraging, individual members of the Church community — especially the sick and the poor;
9. overseeing the community's wider attempt to meet the needs of its members, and of the wider realm in which their

lives are set. (Here the priest will naturally find himself in relation to the deacon.)

Perusal of these nine points will show that the first trio define the content of the *prophetic* office of the presbyter; the second trio of his *priestly* office, and the third of his *pastoral* office. Reference to the bishop and the deacon remind us that the presbyterate cannot be divorced from the episcopate and diaconate, since there is one sacrament of Order in three grades. This is a *triune* sacrament. Within this pattern, each element informs the others, though the heart of it all, the offering of the Mass, is their common centre, which feeds them all.

The difficulty which some evidently have at the present time of conceiving the 'pattern' of the priestly life can be related to the frequently expressed regret of Pope John Paul II that the Second Vatican Council was not subsequently exemplified in the lives of outstanding, paradigmatic priestly saints — such as, in the wake of the Council of Trent, St Vincent de Paul. Such exemplary persons, living classics, embody a theological vision of the priesthood, as of the sacrament of Order as a whole, better than any text. Consolingly, we can remember how protracted was the process of practical 'reception' of that earlier Council — owing to the resistance offered by the powers all Christians foreswear in baptism; the world, the flesh and the devil. Those powers subsist, though their manifestations vary. And so the seed falls, but the garnering of the ripened fruit needs patience.

Appendix

Two Disputed Questions

1. The ordination of women

As we saw when looking at the medieval theology of Order,
the Scholastic theologians had already discussed the question
of why women may not be recipients of this sacrament. Such
conscious affirmations of the inappropriateness of conferring
Order on women are found, indeed, a good deal earlier than
the Middle Ages. In the *Apostolic Church Order*, an Egyptian
work of around the year 300, we read:

> When the Master prayed over the bread and
> the cup and blessed them, saying: 'This is
> my Body and Blood', he did not allow women
> to stand with us.[1]

The negative wording of this text is more happily replaced by
positive language which brings out something of its rationale.
The Church ordains only males; that is, as the Anglican
theologian E.L. Mascall has pointed out: in the Church, Christ
exercises his priesthood ministerially through human beings
who possess human nature in the same sexual mode in which
he possesses it.[2]

The arguments in favour of this aspect of the Church's
practice are, as found nowadays, basically twofold. The first
is the *argument from tradition*. The Vincentian canon, the rule
for assessing doctrinal disputes put forward by the fifth-century
Church father Vincent of Lérins, states that we should hold
fast to

> what has been believed everywhere, always,
> by everyone.[3]

Though there are many difficulties in applying this canon,
nevertheless, as one Orthodox writer has written:

> If ever there was a practice that contravened the
> Vincentian canon, it is certainly the ordination of women
> to the priesthood.[4]

Christ, the apostles, apostolic men, and the local presidents in
the early Church, as well as their episcopal and presbyteral
successors were men and not women. Admittedly, faithfulness
to tradition entails a willingness to discriminate between what
is essential in the inheritance we have received from the
Church's past, and what, by contrast, is contingent. Tradition
is received and lived out by each generation in its own way,
being enriched by the fresh experience that the Church is
constantly gaining. Yet if there is dynamism in tradition there
is also continuity. The Holy Spirit does not bring a new
revelation in the course of the post-apostolic history of the
Church: he brings the everlasting and changeless truth of Christ
himself. As Vincent puts it: *Nove, non nova.* We are to do not
'new things', for the revelation brought by Christ is final,
definitive; yet we are to express Christ's teaching 'in a new
way'. And while Jesus never *said* anything about the ordination
of women, that is, about their participation in the apostolic
ministry his actions speak for themselves. As a Calvinist divine
has said:

> The New Testament, in spite of the chance of total
> renewal which it provides for women as well as for men,
> never testifies that a woman could be, in a public and
> authorised way, the representative of Christ....[5]

It is true, of course, that the apostles Jesus chose were not only
males, but were also circumcised Jews. Almost at once, though,
in the lifetime of the apostles themselves, the Church, in the
persons of the apostles and their associates, decreed circumcision
and other requirements of the Jewish ceremonial law to be no
longer binding on Christians. All apostolic ministry was
henceforth to be open to Jews and Gentiles indifferently. The
apostles did not, however, admit women to the apostolic office,
nor to the ranks of the local ministers they established. The

relevance of this is that it would generally be agreed that decisions or determinations radically constitutive of the Church's structure could be made by the apostles, by the apostolic generation, in a way that could not happen subsequently, after the apostles and their contemporaries had disappeared from the scene. The apostles shared in the gracious authority of the Origin of the Church. The unique nature of the authority of their generation, something most clearly evidenced in the production of the New Testament writings as the plenary witness to the truth of the Gospel, was just that — unique. The freedom which the apostles enjoyed at the 'Jerusalem council' of Acts 13 to modify the pattern of the Church's life as received from its Founder, is not, then, a freedom which the episcopate today may claim for itself. And as the Roman 'Instruction' on the ordination of women, *Inter insigniores,* puts it: this is said not by way of archaism, but of fidelity, of faithfulness to the apostolic tradition.

But it may be asked: even accepting that the apostles had a freedom which we today lack, might not the ordination of women be made possible by appeal to the idea of doctrinal development? In other words: could it not be said that, although a possible sharing of women in the apostolic ministry is not itself a notion found explicitly in the apostolic age, it may nevertheless be teased out of an *implicit* apostolic experience or witness thanks to the ingenuity of the later Church. One starting point for the exercise of such ingenuity might be, for instance, the fact recorded in the Gospel of John that the apostles received the news of the Resurrection (at least in the Johannine version of the story) from Mary Magdalene, whom some early writers therefore call *apostola:* the 'apostle' of the apostles. This is a point: but to it the reply may be made that in a Catholic setting, as in that of the separated Eastern Christians and of many Anglicans, Scripture must be considered by us today not in an exclusive fashion, overleaping the intervening centuries, but in the context of twenty centuries of interpretation. More especially, the idea of doctrinal development presupposes what John Henry Newman, still its most prestigious exponent, termed 'early anticipation'.[6] There are indeed developments in the Church's theory and practice, both in faith and morals, which came late to full recognition. Yet such matters as the prohibition of slavery or the dogmatisation of Mary's immaculate conception do not lack a good deal of such early anticipation — by way of, for example, the writings of individual Church fathers or the evidence of liturgical cultus. By contrast, the ordination of women to the presbyterate and episcopate would be, as all reputable historians admit, a sudden and unprecedented eruption which could not be made sense of in terms of Newman's theory of development or of anything remotely like it.

The argument from tradition is, however, no longer sufficient in itself for many in the historic Christian churches today. Part of the reason why this is so is surely a weakening in the sense of the Church as a supernatural, Spirit-guided reality, in history but not of history, and the growth, conversely, of a tendency to view her as just another institution — though one of, obviously, vital interest to Christians. But leaving this very serious crisis in the sense of faith to one side, in itself there is nothing illegitimate in asking after the why and the wherefore of some aspect of tradition. Indeed, theology might well be defined as the attempt to describe the intelligibility, or intrinsic significance, of tradition. If, then, we go on to ask why women have not been called by the Church to the presbyterate or episcopate, the answer is generally deemed to lie in the second main argument found in connection with the ordination of women, namely, *the argument from the 'iconic' (image-like) character of the ministerial priesthood.*

That the early Church possessed *some* doctrine of this kind — abstracting for the moment from the question of an emphasis on maleness — is not in doubt. As Cyprian of Carthage wrote around the turn of the third and fourth centuries:

> Our Lord and God Jesus Christ is himself the high priest of God the Father; he offered himself as a sacrifice to the Father; and commanded that this should be done in

memory of him. Thus, the priest truly acts in the place of Christ, *vice Christi.*[7]

Again, a seventh-century writer, Antiochus (fl.620), a monk of Mar Saba and active therefore in the (Palestinian) East, rather than the West, had this to say:

> The priests should be imitators of their highpriest (i.e. the bishop), and he in his turn should be an imitator of Christ the high priest.[8]

In a final example, the slightly later Byzantine writer Theodore of Studios (759-826), specifically calls the ministerial priest *hê eikôn tou Christou,* the 'icon of Christ'.[9] But what is the bearing on our subject of this idea of the iconic, representative or 'mimetic' character of the ordained minister *vis-à-vis* Christ? Here it is customary to introduce the thought of the *particularity* of the Incarnation. Certainly, Christ is saviour of all humanity, of men and women equally. But at his incarnation Christ became a particular human being, and, as such, he could not be both male and female at once. And in fact, he was a male. As another Orthodox writer, M. Aghiorgoussis, has put it:

> The ordination of women to the holy priesthood is untenable, since it would disregard the symbolic and iconic value of male priesthood, both as representing Christ's malehood and the fatherly role of the Father in the Trinity by allowing female persons to interchange with male persons a role which cannot be interchanged.[10]

The question which arises here is whether the common term of these relationships, the Father to Christ the Son, and Christ the Son to the male ministerial priest — that is, the common term of *maleness* — is truly necessary, not just in terms of what the patristic writers quoted above may have intended, but what is the case in and of itself for those who wish to be faithful to the Christian revelation.

A Lutheran author has argued persuasively in this connection that Trinitarian 'Father'-language cannot be dismissed as a piece of male sexism, and that those who do so dismiss it reflect what he terms a 'breakdown of linguistic and doctrinal information and sophistication'. The question Robert Jenson raises is, Was it just an accident that divine revelation took place in a society which tended to use the masculine gender for God, a tendency which revelation, in most respects, overwhelmingly confirmed? Was it by caprice, that God did *not* use as his vehicle a society with a predominantly female religious symbolism, or one with a symbolism which was ambivalently male and female together, even though both of these types of religious culture existed in the ancient world? That it was not such a fluke has to do, in the first place, with God's relation to the world. We can approach this point by asking, Is the world *born* of God? or is it *willed* by God? Is the world the offspring of God, an emanation of God? Is everything in us and about us a manifestation of God, as pantheists say? Or, is the world the work of God, something distinct from himself, discontinuous with him, willed as a whole, but with some aspects willed only conditionally, in so far as they are required, or may be, by other aspects which are willed unconditionally, so that the world is not in every respect a good guide to what God is like? The people of Israel opted decisively for the second of these two positions.

> It is decisive for Israel's God that his filial relation to us is established only by his sheer will, that is, that his role as our parent is not sexual, that he is not even metaphorically a fertility god.[11]

Faced with having to select between 'Mother' or 'Father' as the proper name of God — as one must, since 'parent' by itself does not individuate—the criterion should be which name is the more easily separated from its function as the name of a role in our bisexual reproduction. Once this criterion is adopted, it becomes clear that only 'Father' will do, since 'Mother' is too intimately involved with the process of reproduction. In other words, a mother goddess is too continuous with the world, too much like the womb from which we came, to stand for the divine reality revealed in the Old Testament, a reality that is decisively other than the world, different from the world, discontinuous with the world, and with a plan, indeed, for the world's remaking.[12]

Secondly, the primacy of male gender symbolism in our religion also has to do with the relation between the Father (as, with the Old Testament, we may now call the only God) and the *Word* — the eternal expression of the Father who, in the New Testament, becomes incarnate as Jesus Christ. What the Word comes forth from is one single source, not a co-operative enterprise involving a begetter and a bearer. And here again, the origin of the Word has to be described, therefore, by that gender language which can more easily be detached from our experience of reproduction. And so the New Testament confirms the intuition of the Old that the primary gender symbolism for God must be male: *Abba,* 'dear Father', as Jesus calls him in his private prayer; of which prayer the Lord's Prayer is the public formulation for the use of disciples — the *Our Father.* Once 'Father' is recognised in this way as the proper name of God, then it becomes quite feasible to use female symbolism in a secondary, metaphorical way: to describe God's care and loving kindness as that of a mother for her children; or, in Christ's own words about himself, as a mother-hen gathering her chicks beneath her wings. Thus, for Thomas Aquinas, the 'proper' names of Father, Son and Holy Spirit are literally applicable to God, resting as they do on the inter-relationship of the divine persons to each other, whereas any other names are analogical or metaphorical, depending for what justification they may have on an experience of the created medium.[13]

When in Jesus Christ the Word of God becomes human as a male, the Redeemer reflects what we have just seen about the Creator. A male Redeemer better represents the difference of God from the world, and so the action of God *vis-à-vis* the world, and therefore the difference which this action can make to the world. In orthodox Christianity, accordingly, the male principle provides the symbolism for the divine action, whereas the female principle furnishes the symbolism for the context or conditions of that action.[14] Through Mary's *fiat,* that principle provides the 'matrix' — the source, condition, context — of the incarnational and sacramental principles. And this is intelligible, since the female is, through her bio-rhythms, and their psychological resonances and analogies, more closely linked than is the male to what is material and bodily. Jesus has no human father, but through his mother he expresses the divine Word in the finite, and especially, in the flesh. Similarly, it is suggested, through the Church, as Bride of Christ, eternally feminine *vis-à-vis* him, souls are brought into a relationship with Jesus which Scripture describes in terms of a marriage-covenant. Thus the role of Mary and of the Church, both Bride and Mother, which Mary typifies, is to provide the conditions and context of extended sacramentality within which Christ acts both in his public ministry and in the ministerial priesthood which is the continuation *par excellence* of his own ministerial action. The female principle, in providing the conditions of the incarnation and of the sacramental life can be correlated with the economy of the Holy Spirit, by which Jesus' humanity was anointed, or prepared, at the Annunciation for the hypostatic union, and by which also the Church was first brought into being at Pentecost as Bride and Mother. The male principle, equal but complementary, represents and *re*-presents Christ's saving action, and so can be correlated with the economy of the Son, who, as Incarnate in our humanity, receives the Spirit before giving him. Curiously enough, this typology is already established, or so it seems, in the ancient Syrian text known as the *Didascalia Apostolorum,* in just our context of ministry. There we read:

> The deacon is in the place of Christ, and you will love him. You will honour the deaconesses in the place of the Spirit.[15]

The apostolic ministry mediates the Son in his historical maleness; the Church community, typologically female, mediates the Spirit. It is notable that Protestant objections to the restriction of the ordained ministry to males in the Catholic tradition sometimes turn on a denial of the very principle of such ecclesial mediation of God in Christ. Thus the American Protestant exegete Samuel Terrien has written:

> As long as a male priest claims that he re-enacts in a sacramental form the sacrifice of Jesus on the Cross and is thereby identified mystically with the living Christ — the Bridegroom of the Church — any discussion on the ordination of women will remain sterile.[16]

In other words: first abandon the notion of a sacramental mediation of Christ as High Priest of the Eucharistic sacrifice — and then we shall be able to agree on the gender of the ordained! But this would be to overthrow the Eucharistic doctrine of the Church, in both East and West.

In what concrete ways, then, can women serve the Church? An account of the total pattern of the Church's ministry exceeds the limitations of this book which studies simply the theology of ordination. Such an account would belong more properly to an investigation of the sacraments of initiation, by which the royal and prophetic priesthood of the faithful is constituted. To answer the question, Can women be presbyters and bishops? in the negative still leaves open the questions, What are the distinctive gifts conferred by God on women? and How can those gifts be expressed in the Church's life and action? Much current propaganda for the ordination of women envisages the priesthood, whether presbyteral or episcopal, as virtually the only possible form of significant service to the wider Church. Thus the present campaign for women's ordination has been called by one French Orthodox lay observer, 'the bitter fruit of the clericalisation of the Church'.[17]

The Catholic Church is considering, at the present time, the advantages and disadvantages of putting in place a considerable number of 'instituted' and or 'commissioned' lay ministries — based, then, on the sacraments of Christian initiation — in order to provide counter-balancing analogies to the male ordained ministries of the ministerial priesthood and diaconate.[18] The current 'explosion' of ministries is, in fact, remarkably akin to the development of minor orders in the patristic Church. It has the merit of underlining the fact that the life and action of the Church take many forms other than those of the apostolic ministry. Yet it also has demerits. The most potentially damaging of these is the possible implication that only those lay (and in our context more specifically female) contributions to the Church's life and action capable of formalisation as 'ministries' are worthwhile. However, the Catholic laity, both female and male, carry out innumerable services to the Gospel, both as regards their fellow believers in the household of faith, and as regards non-Catholic Christians, and non-Christians *tout court,* and these services far exceed, in both quantity and variety, what it would be practicable to formalise as instituted ministries. Husband and father, wife and mother; friend and neighbour; colleague and associate: all of this is the sphere of the ordinary Christian life (which *au fond* is supernaturally *extra*ordinary) yet resists encapsulation in institutional terms. There is also that wide and variegated canvas: the world of politics and social charity; of work and professions; of culture and the arts; of recreation and hobbies where, in the past, Catholic societies have flourished, enhancing both fellowship and mission. In quantity and quality, these modes of action, directed either towards the common life of the Church ('lay ministry') or at the world beyond ('the lay apostolate') will always exceed in importance any development of formalised roles. To attempt to formalise them all would be, not only a waste of administrative energy, but an unparalleled exercise in para-liturgical pomposity: thus the 'grass-cutting ministry' of the lad in the American churchyard described by the Vaticanologist Peter Hebblethwaite![19]

If the word 'ministry' is to be used of lay activity, it should be employed, I suggest, in a similar fashion to the use of the term 'apostolate' in such movements of the 1920s and afterwards as 'Catholic Action'. That is, just as the *action* of the apostolic ministry towards the world in proclaiming the Gospel has its lay analogue in the parallel efforts of the Catholic laity to do the same, so the life of the apostolic ministry, as the building up of the common life of the Church, has *its* lay analogues in the myriad contributions that the Catholic people make to the life of parish, diocese, universal Church: their 'ministry'. But we should recognise here that, just as many members of the laity have always been 'apostolic', whether they have used that term or not, as many or more have been 'ministerial' in their enhancement of the Church's life, even though the *word* would, no doubt, have sounded to them technical and strange.

To insist on formalisation and institutionalisation of such apostolic action and ministerial life would be to inhibit the initiative-taking and self-organising qualities which the Catholic laity should continue to develop for the effective promotion of the faith and the growth of the Church as a communion of charity. Only those aspects of their activity which *need* to be so formalised and institutionalised should be thus treated. This means, I believe, those which form part of the Church's regular worship, the daily and weekly staple, of her most fundamental action, the Liturgy. This is precisely what we have seen so far, with the creation of such 'offices' as lector, acolyte, and extraordinary minister of Holy Communion. Are there specifically female possibilities here?

One possibility is a revival of the ancient office of deaconesses, an office whose functions included at any rate in the Christian East, the preparation of women for the catechumenate and baptism; the instruction of children and adolescents; certain liturgical functions, and the care of women who are sick. In the West, deaconnesses were less common, and had somewhat ill-defined liturgical functions, usually in monasteries.[20] Such deaconnesses seem to have disappeared in both East and West at roughly the same time, the eleventh century. There can be no theological objection to the revival of such an office. There is, however, a danger of archaising if a ministry for which no clear need is perceived were re-created simply because it was patristic![21]

It is a moot point just how the order of deaconesses should be related to that of deacons. The general assumption is that the deaconess is the non-sacramental counterpart of the deacon.

> The rites situate their ministry within the tradition of the holy women of Israel, rather than within the apostolic charge.[22]

But granted that there is, in modern Catholic teaching, a major difference between the diaconal and the presbyteral-episcopal ministries — the former being its own sacramental mode of assistance to the bishop rather than a participation in *his* sacrament — might it be feasible to regard deaconesses as genuinely women deacons, while maintaining the position that they cannot be called to the *sacerdotium* of presbyter and bishop for the reasons outlined above?[23] It is difficult not to think that the creation of women deacons would call into question the unity of the sacrament of Order. In so far as that sacrament represents the work of Christ as Head in the Church, moreover, its symbolism is naturally male, even when the *munus sacerdotale* in its full form of a sacrificing priesthood is not at stake.

Another form of relationship between women and the sacrament of Order is that constituted by the role of wives. The topic of the wives of Western deacons is beginning to receive some exploration. More significant in the past of the Eastern churches has been the role of the presbyter's wife: *presbytera* or *pappadia* in Greek, *matushka,* 'little mother', to the priest's *babushka,* 'little father', in Russian and Ukrainian. The idea behind these terms is that the spiritual fatherhood exercised by the priest is mirrored in a spiritual motherhood (once again) exercised by his wife. This suggestion raises the wider issue of the discipline of presbyteral celibacy in the Church, to which we must now turn.

2. Priesthood and celibacy

The *history* of priestly celibacy is a controverted topic which still awaits its definitive chronicling, especially where the claim to an apostolic origin is concerned. According to the view until recently 'in possession', there was in the early Church no law of celibacy as such: celibacy was favoured, yet remained an optional discipline. In the fourth century, however, and notably, so far as the West is concerned, at the Spanish council of Elvira (c. 305), it came to be insisted that an ordained man who was married should henceforth live in permanent, unconditional continence 'as a sign and consequence of his new consecration as a minister of the Church'.[24] In the West, regional councils, including Roman ones, had mixed successes in their attempts to introduce this notion during the patristic period. Only with the Gregorian reform of the eleventh and twelfth centuries was the discipline effectively established over large areas of the Latin church.[25] In the East, by contrast, whilst the same tendency made itself felt — for example, at the Council of Nicaea — it was resisted;[26] the acts of the late seventh-century Byzantine council *in Trullo,* which accepted a married presbyterate, would there mark its definitive retreat.

A movement of revisionist historiography, however, has of late challenged this thesis, and sought to reinstitute the claims of an earlier generation of divines that the law of celibacy is apostolic in origin — and thus stands at the source of the experience of the ordained ministry not only in the West but also in the East. Thus Christian Cochini, of the Society of Jesus,[27] takes with considerable seriousness the words of an episcopal speaker at the little-studied council of Carthage of 390:

> It is proper that the sacred bishops, priests of God as well as deacons, or those who are at the service of the divine sacraments, should be absolutely continent in order to obtain in all simplicity what they ask for from God: so that what the apostles taught and antiquity itself has observed we might also observe ....[28]

Although the Fathers differed in their assessment as to which apostles were unmarried, and which married, they agreed, so Father Roman Cholij of the Ukrainian Catholic exarchate of

Great Britain informs us, in attesting that such apostles as had wives lived in a condition of conjugal abstinence,[29] taking their cue from the words of the Lord reported in Luke 18:28-30:

> Truly I say to you, there is no man who has left house or wife or brothers or parents or children for the sake of the kingdom of God, who will not receive more in this time, and in the age to come eternal life.

One might add that, for Clement of Alexandria, Epiphanius of Salamis and John Chrysostom, just as important is 1 Corinthians 7:5 and 32-35, where Paul recommends abstinence from conjugal union for 'seasons of prayer' and, in general, for the more undivided prosecution of the 'affairs of the Lord'.[30] For Epiphanius, where the Church's rule is strictly kept, not only bishops and presbyters but even deacons and sub-deacons are celibate, or at least keep continence, since the Church considers that

> those who celebrate divine worship should not be distracted from it but should perform their duties with a conscience perfectly disposed.[31]

By an *a fortiori* argument, if the Corinthian laity are to practise periodic continence on spiritual grounds, how much more should continence be kept by priests. Though conclusive evidence is lacking, it seems likely that those bishops and priests (perhaps deacons and sub-deacons too) who, on ordination were married men, would have expected to live continently afterwards.

The early Byzantine council *in Trullo,* summoned in 691-692 by the emperor Justinian II, departed from this earlier shared tradition which, if not universal, was at the very least widespread, by permitting the use of marriage to presbyters, deacons and sub-deacons — though only at times when they were not preparing to celebrate the Eucharistic Mysteries. As The council remarks, citing its predecessor at Carthage, already mentioned:

> Subdeacons who wait upon the Holy Mysteries, and deacons and presbyters, should abstain from their spouses during the periods particularly assigned to them, so that what has been handed down through the apostles and preserved by ancient custom, we too likewise maintain, knowing that there is a time for all things and especially for fasting and prayer. For it is proper that they who assist at the divine altar should be absolutely continent when they are handling holy things, in order to obtain in all simplicity what they ask for from God.[32]

In point of fact, the Greek drafters of Canon 13 of Trullo, in which these words appear, modified the Latin original of Carthage to reduce *permanent* continence to *temporary*. The norms which the Council *in Trullo* put in place did not imply, it should be noted, any more than had the earlier more comprehensive maxims, any contempt for the conjugal act. Rather did they have the nature of a pre-Eucharistic fast, as the text itself makes plain. However, they did have the unfortunate effect of introducing what Cholij terms a 'levitical' colouring into the presentation of the priestly office: the presbyters (and other clerics) of Trullo are, so far as Eucharistic practice is concerned, part-time ministers who succeed each other in a rota of temporary duties.

> Trullo itself, by changing the celibacy praxis of Carthage, which was consistent with doctrine, unwittingly prepared the way for a change (at least in emphasis) in the very theology of the priesthood: from an ontological category to a functional one. In the fourth century, on the other hand, it was precisely the emphasis on the priesthood being considered as a continual and uninterrupted ministry that provided an argument for perpetual continence.[33]

As a number of Western texts, and notably early papal decretals make clear, the priest is, by virtue of his vocation, perpetually 'on call'.

Cholij shows that, in Orthodoxy, the growing tendency to

treat the 'indulgence' of the Trullan canon 13 as, in effect, a precept, led to a number of strange results. These include the insistence on prior marriage for the non-monastic clergy; the dismissal of priests whose wives predecease them; and the inability of Orthodox canonists and theologians to offer a rationale for the prohibition of a second marriage for clerics (the 'husband of one wife' — only — of the Pastoral Letters), or even of the (first) marriage of one already ordained. Moreover, the reception of the decrees of Trullo by such influential Western canonists as Gratian disabled the subsequent Latin tradition from arguing — as otherwise it surely would have — for the apostolic origin of celibacy, or dedicated continence, as a demand arising from the very nature of the ministerial priesthood itself. The canon would create difficulties when, as in many places (at least in the Oriental Churches in union with Rome), the faithful came to desire more frequent, and even daily, celebrations of the Liturgy.

> The only possible solution to the increasing demands of more frequent celebration while maintaining the thousand year old Oriental discipline on priestly continence was to increase the number of strict celibates. Celibacy, it was true, was desirable on other accounts too, but this disciplinary conflict was undoubtedly a very significant factor in the movement to introduce celibacy in the Oriental Catholic churches ....

And so, Cholij concludes,

> The Oriental Catholic Churches of the nineteenth and twentieth centuries, in introducing celibacy, were but catching up on history. Celibacy is not a Latinisation. It is a true orientalisation. It is refinding the roots.[34]

Theologically, a good deal can be said in favour of linking the charism of celibacy with ministerial office. Schillebeeckx, in an early study, calls the Western law of celibacy the juridical formulation of the 'inner logic of a particular religious experience'.[35] The experience he has in mind is that of the

159

apostles themselves, as implied by the Synoptic tradition.

> The gift of the coming Kingdom held them so in its spell
> that they left everything joyfully and without counting
> the cost; it was not even possible now for them to go back
> to their married lives. They could no longer devote
> themselves to goods and possessions. They could no
> longer concern themselves with their own livelihood. It
> was a matter of existentially not being able to do
> otherwise. In this sense they are truly 'eunuchs'. There
> are such people, says Jesus. Clearly, this applies to the
> apostles.[36]

And we may add here that, just as the mission of the apostles
is founded on, and patterned after, that of the Son sent from
the Father, so their celibacy cannot be left unrelated to that
of Jesus himself — even though the Lord's own all-absorbing
dedication to his task, vis-à-vis the Father's and vis-à-vis
human beings at large, is not explicitly referred by the New
Testament to his unmarried state. The ultimate foundation for
celibacy can only be, as *Presbyterorum ordinis* 16 insists, and Pope
Paul VI's letter on priestly celibacy reiterates, 'the mystery of
Christ and his mission'.

That letter, *Sacerdotalis caelibatus* of 1967, not only echoes
Tradition in drawing out, from the tacit dimension of the
Scriptures, an explicit connection between the celibacy of Jesus
and his redemptive work. It also completes the purification of
the same Tradition from various influences of an extra-
evangelical kind operative in the early Church. The most
notable among the latter were: the ideal of ritual continence
in the pagan cults of Greece and Rome; the rejection of sexual
pleasure in Stoic philosophy; and the depreciation of the body
in neo-Platonism and neo-Pythagoreanism.[37] For the pope
refuses to speak of ministerial celibacy without, in the same
breath, celebrating the transfiguration of marriage by the grace
of Christ.

Marriage, which, by God's will, continues the work of the first creation, taken up into the total design of salvation, also acquires (with the Redemption) a new meaning and value. Jesus, in fact, has re-established its primordial dignity, honoured it and raised it to the dignity of a sacrament and mysterious sign of his union with the Church.... But Christ, as Mediator of a yet more excellent Covenant, opened, too, a new way, in which the human creature, adhering totally and directly to the Lord, and preoccupied solely with him and his affairs, manifests in a clearer and more complete manner the profoundly innovatory reality of the New Testament.[38]

And Pope Paul explains that, if the apostolic ministry be a unique sharing in Christ's priesthood, it must involve a dedication to his saving mission of a kind which mirrors the 'form of charity and sacrifice' proper to the Redeemer, wherein his freedom from the ties of flesh and blood is part. Or as the early Schillebeeckx puts it, underlining the appropriateness of linking celibacy to Church office in the case of those who continue the apostles' ministry in the later community:

> On the basis of the biblical connection between religious celibacy and the Kingdom of God, she (the Church) has concretised the state of life of all who wish freely to accept office in the Church into a Christian way of life that made them, because of an intimate love of God, available to all in a special way, without a binding relationship to one person.[39]

In the course of time, by reflecting more deeply on the nature of this 'biblical connection', the Church, both Eastern and Western, decided to restrict its choice of bishops to celibates, or to those willing to accept the venture of celibacy. This remains today the practice of the Catholic, Orthodox, 'Oriental Orthodox' and 'Assyrian' churches.

As the bishop is the principal inheritor of the apostolic ministry it was indeed natural that the link between episcopate and celibacy should be discovered first. Since that time, the Church has increasingly been coming to the conclusion that the same link holds good for the other order which has inherited a major share via the episcopate in the apostolic ministry — namely, the presbyterate. This is really a case of development not of doctrine *tout court* but of doctrinally-based discipline. Though it holds good mainly for the Western Church, signs of it can be detected in the East as well. Whereas the law of celibacy is a Latin creation, the Catholic East has, in practice, and not solely under the influence of the Latin rite, given ever more scope to a celibate priesthood.

A celibate presbyterate and a married presbyterate are not, then, or so it would seem, theologically equal options. The general direction of developing insight in the Church since the patristic period is to link celibacy with the presbyterate, just as the patristic Church had linked it with the episcopate, and for precisely the same reasons. That is, if the presbyterate is, via the episcopate, truly an apostolic ministry — a ministry not simply founded by the apostles but inheriting a share in their own ministry itself, then it should ideally be as celibate as apostleship and episcopate themselves. From this viewpoint, the situation of the separated Eastern Churches is one where what looks suspiciously like development of doctrinally-based discipline has not come to its full term. Although there is, in the words of John Henry Newman, 'early anticipation' of a celibate Eastern clergy in the Oriental practice of asking dedicated continence from presbyters (and deacons), the Eastern Churches have not as yet found in that early anticipation a key to what might be their own practice today. In this, they must be allowed their own freedom to move at their own pace; and indeed, to indicate to the Latin Church whether its own tradition of presbyteral celibacy is a harbinger of the universal future or not. Meanwhile, in Raymond Brown's words,

> Precisely because the witness of celibacy is conspicuously lacking in many other Christian churches, the Roman Catholic Church has an ecumenical duty to the Gospel

162

to continue to bear an effective witness on this score.

And Brown adds:

> Perhaps this would be possible without a law, but one
> must admit that it is the law of priestly celibacy that makes
> it clear that those who accept it are doing so for the sake
> of Christ and not simply because they prefer to be
> bachelors. Some of the forms of optional celibacy being
> proposed would soon lead to obscuring the vocational
> character of celibacy and would reduce it to a personal
> idiosyncracy.[40]

As Cardinal Jean-Marie Lustiger of Paris has insisted, the
historic decision of the Latin Church to enforce the extension
of ministerial celibacy from the episcopate to the entire Western
priesthood was not a practical matter, but rather a commitment
to a certain type of ministerial holiness.

> The spiritual choice of the Western church is thus not to
> link priestly ordination with mere pastoral needs that
> could be tallied and projected by statistics. (This) enables
> us, paradoxically, to give way to a logic of graciousness,
> that is, of grace — since God does not reason in a
> technocratic way — to transform the number of
> ordinations from an administrative decision into a gift of
> faith.[41]

For, as another contemporary hierarch, Archbishop Francis
Stafford of Denver, has written, priestly celibacy has in the
last analysis, a *mystical* meaning. Commenting on the teaching
of *Presbyterorum ordinis*(16) that celibate presbyters become better
fitted thereby for 'a broader acceptance of fatherhood in Christ',
Stafford has this to say:

> Since Christ was unmarried, we may find it strange at
> first that the Council speaks of fatherhood in Christ. Yet
> the hymn *Summi Parentis Filio* speaks of Christ as father
> of the world to come. If we bear in mind what St Paul
> teaches us about the spousal love of Christ for his Church,

163

we will see that this 'world to come' is nothing less than the child of that union, the fruit of that love.... It is not for nothing that the priest is addressed as 'Father' by his people.

As with the fatherhood of Christ, that of the priest points to the world to come: his solitude and earthly barrenness, a prefiguring of death; his prayer, pastoral charity and spiritual fruitfulness, a sign of God's power which is at work now to sanctify and so to yield eternal life.[42]

It is at this level of depth that the historic option of the Catholic Church for a celibate presbyterate, at least in her predominant portion, the partriarchate of the West, must be approached.

On the other hand, this affirmation of the general preferability of a celibate presbyterate is compatible with the acceptance of an auxiliary married presbyterate *in certain cases.* For particular situations and purposes, such an auxiliary married priesthood might be helpful in the Latin Church itself. These particular situations and purposes should, to my mind, be *highly* particular — an example might be where a movement such as Marriage Encounter is organised on a systematic basis with a network of full-time chaplains. This should be distinguished from a generalised abolition of the link between the presbyterate and celibacy for particular churches, i.e. for particular areas of the world. To say that local churches, in given parts of the globe, cannot be expected to produce celibate ministers of the Gospel is to say that they cannot be expected to reproduce an intrinsic element in the experience of the apostles. And this seems a strange way in which to recognise the Christian maturity of such churches!

This position is, then, in different respects more rigorist and less rigorist than that of present-day Church discipline. However, I make no claims to be a prophet of the future of the 'brotherhood of holy pastors' (Newman's phrase) which the sacrament of Order creates in the Church. This much may yet be said: that future, if it is to be genuinely Catholic, must be in manifest continuity with what has gone before. In an age where journalism often replaces scholarship in the Church, not least in its deliberate creation of opinion, and when Church leaders sometimes resemble political pundits in feeling that they must always have 'solutions' for everything, the need to stress the principle of tradition as foundational to the Catholic idea is especially great today.

Notes

Chapter 1: The Apostolic Ministry in the New Testament

1. J.H. Newman, 'The Christian Ministry', in *Parochial and Plain Sermons* (London 1880), pp. 300-319, and here at p. 304.
2. Ibid., p. 301.
3. cf. G. Bornkamm, *Paul* (ET London, 1971, 1975), pp. xi, 26; for Paul's dependence on tradition, see F.F. Bruce, *Paul: Apostle of the Free Spirit* (Exeter 1977), pp. 83-93.
4. The Jewish background of this notion is discussed in P. Borgen, 'God's Agent in the Fourth Gospel', in idem., *Logos was the True Light* (Trondheim 1983), pp. 121-132, and especially pp. 122-128.
5. The phrase was coined by Theo Preiss in idem., *Life in Christ* (London 1954), p. 25.
6. J. Galot, *Theology of the Priesthood* (ET San Francisco 1985), pp. 45-48.
7. A. Feuillet, *The Priesthood of Christ and His Ministers* (ET New York 1975).
8. R.E. Brown, SS, *Priest and Bishop, Biblical Reflections* (London 1970), pp. 10-13. Usefully, Brown reminds his readers that the existence of a specialised priesthood in ancient Israel was not deemed to be incompatible with calling the entire nation a 'kingdom of priests, a holy nation' *(Ex 19:6)*, ibid., p.7.
9. 1 Clement 40.
10. The statement of Hebrews that the ministry of the high-priestly Christ is one of mediation of the new Covenant (8,6 *mesitês*) has been understood in Church tradition as the confession of a unique reality which is yet open to participation: see A. Vanhoye, SJ., *Prêtres ancien, prêtre nouveau selon le Nouveau Testament* (Paris 1980), conclusion.
11. M. Thurian, *Priesthood and Ministry, Ecumenical Research* (ET London 1983), pp. 41-42.
12. *Presbeuô*, to act as an ambassador *(presbeutês)* appears to enjoy a relationship with *presbuteros*, presbyter, 'priest', thus giving the latter a connotation of representative legateship echoing (albeit faintly) that of 'apostle' itself.
13. B. Kloppenburg, OFM, *The Priest, Living Instrument and Minister of Christ the Eternal Priest* (ET Chicago 1974), p. 51.
14. M. Thurian, *Priesthood and Ministry*, op. cit., p. 55.
15. Irenaeus, *Adversus haereses* III.12.10.
16. See the section on *'Presbyteroi* in the Local and Synagogal Government of Hellenistic Judaism' in G. Bornkamm, *'Presbys, presbyteros, sympresbyteros, presbyterion'*, in G. Kittel and G. Friedrich (eds.), *Theological Dictionary of the New Testament* IV (ET Grand Rapids, Michigan 1968), pp. 651-680.
17. On James as a 'prototype of the monarchical bishop of succeeding generations', see J. A. Mohler, SJ, *The Origin and Evolution of the Priesthood, A Return to the Sources* (Staten Island, New York 1970), p. 17.

18. Papias of Hierapolis (c. 60-130) speaks of a certain 'John the Presbyter' in a fragment of his lost 'Expositions of the Oracles of the Lord', preserved in Eusebius' *Church History* at II. 39, 4. On this, see J. Munck, 'Presbyters and Disciples of the Lord in Papias', *Harvard Theological Review* 52 (1959), pp. 223-243. Abbot John Chapman of Downside (and formerly monk of Erdington) tried to assess the relation of Papias' John to the Johannine corpus in 'The Historical Setting of the Second and Third Epistles of Saint John', *Journal of Theological Studies* 5 (1904), pp. 357-368, and 517-534; and in his *John the Presbyter and the Fourth Gospel* (Oxford 1911).

19. *Didache* 15, 1 appears to show their phasing out in favour of a Church order of (presbyter-) bishops and deacons.

20. R.E. Brown, SS, *Priest and Bishop,* op. cit., pp. 67-69.

21. C.K. Barrett, *A Commentary on the First Epistle to the Corinthians* (New York 1968), p. 295.

22. Indeed, in the mid-second-century Roman document, *The Shepherd,* by Hermas, presbyters are specifically called *proïstamenoi tês ekklêsias:* 'Visions', II. 4, 3.

23. See E. Schillebeeckx, *Ministry, A Case for Change* (London 1981); idem., *The Church with a Human Face. A New and Expanded Theology of Ministry* (London 1985).

24. P. Grelot, *Eglise et ministère. Pour un dialogue critique avec Edward Schillebeeckx* (Paris 1983), pp. 27-28.

25. I Clement 42:1-4.

26. J. Colson, *Les Fonctions diaconales aux origines de l'Eglise* (Bruges 1960).

27. See J.M. Barnett, *The Diaconate. A Full and Equal Order* (New York 1979; 1981), p. 38.

28. G. Dix, *The Shape of the Liturgy* (Westminster 1949), p. 28. The arrangement of the elders of the Apocalypse around the throne may reflect the liturgical seating arrangements of such Oriental churches as that of Antioch, described, implicitly, in Ignatius' *To the Magnesians,* 13.

29. A. Farrer, 'The Ministry in the New Testament', in K. E. Kirk (ed.), *The Apostolic Ministry* (London 1946), pp. 113-182.

30. J.A. Mohler, SJ, *The Origin and Evolution of the Priesthood, A Return to the Sources,* op. cit., p. 23.

Chapter 2: The Age of the Fathers

1. G. Dix, 'The Ministry in the Early Church, c. A.D. 90-410', in K.E. Kirk (ed.), *The Apostolic Ministry* (London 1946), pp. 183-303, and here at p. 202.

2. *Adversus Haereses* IV. 26. 2. Cf. W.C. van Unnik, 'The Authority of the Presbyters in Irenaeus' Works', in J. Jervell and W.A. Meeks (eds.), *God's Christ and His People* (Oslo 1977, = N.A. Dahl Festschrift), pp. 248-260.

3. Hegesippus: fragments in Eusebius, *Historia ecclesiastica* IV. 22; Tertullian: *Praescriptio* 20, 32; *Adversus Marcionem* IV. 5.

4. *Traditio apostolica* 3; B. Botte (ed.), *Hippolyte de Rome. La Tradition apostolique* (Paris 1968), p.44.
5. Tertullian: *De baptismo* 17; Cyprian: *Epistolae* 66.
6. *Sarapionis Sacramentarium* 14.
7. *Didascalia Apostolorum* II. 26:4-8.
8. Cf. *To the Smyrnaeans* 8; *To the Philadelphians* 4.
9. *To the Ephesians* 6; cf. ibid., 15; *To the Magnesians* 8.
10. Newman's sermon on 'Order, the Witness and Instrument of Unity' calls Ignatius the Church's pre-eminent 'prophet and doctor ... as regards the structure and the sacramental power of the Ecclesiastical Hierarchy' — an echo, in part, of the convictions of the High Church divines of the Stuart Restoration and their Non-Juring successors after the 'Glorious' Revolution of 1688. see idem., *Sermons Preached on Various Occasions* (1857;1908), pp. 183-198.
11. *To the Trallians* 2 (Christ); ibid., 3 (the Father).
12. e.g., ibid., 2-3; *To the Philadelphians* 5.
13. Cited J. Lécuyer, CSSp, *What is a Priest?* (ET London 1959), pp. 34-35.
14. Ibid., p. 35.
15. *Traditio apostolica* 7; G. Dix, 'The Ministry in the Early Church', art. cit., p. 218.
16. *Epistolae* 5.
17. *To the Smyrnaeans* 8.
18. *Traditio apostolica* 8.
19. *To the Magnesians* 6.
20. G. Dix, 'The Ministry in the Early Church', art. cit., p. 223.
21. This *proestôs* who gives thanks is a major figure in the reconstruction of the development of the ministry offered in A. Afanasieff, *L'Eglise du Saint-Esprit* (Paris 1967). See the present author's *Theology in the Russian Diaspora, Church, Fathers, Eucharist in Nikolai Afanas'ev, 1893-1966* (Cambridge 1989).
22. J.M. Garrigues, M.-J. Le Guillou, A. Riou, 'Le caractère sacerdotale dans la tradition des pères grecs', *Nouvelle Revue Théologique* 93 (1971), pp. 801-820.
23. H. Crouzel, SJ, 'The Ministry in the Church: Reflections on a Recent Publication. II The Witness of the Ancient Church', *Clergy Review* (May 1983), pp. 164-168, 173-174, and here at 167-168.
24. The lengthy period of peace for the Church which characterised the rule of the Syrian Roman emperors, from approximately the death of Septimius Severus in 211 to the accession of Decius in 249, helps to explain this growth, which took place not only in the towns but also (for the first time) in the countryside. See C. H. Turner, 'The Organisation of the Church', in H. M. Gwatkin and J. P. Whitney (eds.), *The Cambridge Mediaeval History I. The Christian Empire* (Cambridge 1911), pp. 143-182.
25. *Epistolae* 146, 1.
26. *Homilia* II. 1 in 1 *Timotheum, 3:8.*

27. Canon 18 of the Council of Nicaea insists — with, evidently, this misunderstanding in mind — that deacons are in fact inferior to presbyters.
28. A. Souter, *A Study of Ambrosiaster* (Cambridge 1905).
29. See T.G. Jalland, 'The Doctrine of the Parity of Ministers', in K. E. Kirk (ed.), *The Apostolic Ministry,* op. cit., pp. 305-350, and here at pp. 312-319. Jalland suggests additionally that the growth of urban churches, the beginnings of rural churches, and the sudden removal of bishops by the civil arm during the Decian persecution were other contributory factors in the rise of presbyteral leadership in this period.
30. *Panarion* LXXV. 3:3.
31. T.G. Jalland, 'The Doctrine of the Parity of Ministers', art. cit.
32. L. Gougaud, *Les Chrétientés celtiques* (Paris 1911), pp. 60-108.
33. Th. Gottlob, *Der abendländische Chorepiskopat* (Bonn 1928), pp. 82-83.
34. S. Ryan, 'Episcopal Consecration: the Legacy of the Schoolmen', *Irish Theological Quarterly* XXXIII. 1 (January 1966), pp. 3-38. However, more recent research into the Irish sources suggests a more fully functioning episcopate: see R. Sharpe, 'Some Problems concerning the Organisation of the Church in Early Mediaeval Ireland', *Peritia* 3 (1984), pp. 230-270.
35. J. Lécuyer, 'Épiscopat et presbytérat dans les écrits d'Hippolyte de Rome', *Recherches de science religieuse* 41 (1953), pp. 30-50.
36. On the introduction of the *cursus honorum,* see L. Ott, *Das Weihesakrament* (Freiburg 1969), pp. 27-28; 42-43. Ott suggests that decisive in this regard was the influence of the gallic *Statuta Ecclesiae antiqua* of c. 400. See on the latter, B. Botte, 'Le rituel d'ordination des *Statuta Ecclesiae antiqua*', *Recherches de théologie ancienne et médiaevale* 11 (1939), pp. 223-241.
37. *Commentarium in Isaiam* 16,58,10.
38. A practice officially sanctioned by the Theodosian Code, promulgated in 438/9 (*Codex Theodosianus* 16.5.26).
39. For the minor orders, see F. Wieland, *Die genetische Entwicklung der sogenannten 'Ordines minores' in den drei ersten Jahrhunderten* (Regensburg 1897); M. Andrieu, 'Les ordres mineurs dans l'ancien rite romain', *Revue des Sciences religieuses* 5 (1925), pp. 232-274.
40. H.A. Wilson, *The Gregorian Sacramentary under Charles the Great* (London 1915), p. 139; cited in L. Ott, *Das Weihesakrament,* op. cit., p. 21.
41. See on this A. Louth, *Denys the Areopagite* (London 1989), pp. 38-43; 65-67.
42. *De baptismo contra Donatistas,* The translation used here is *On Baptism, against the Donatists,* and *The Answer to Letters of Petilian,* in J.R. King (tr.), *Writings in Connection with the Donatist Controversy* (Edinburgh 1872), p. 2.
43. Ibid., p. 3.
44. Ibid.
45. See P. Anson, *Bishops at Large* (London 1964).
46. M. Pellegrino, *The True Priest: the Priesthood as Preached and Practiced by Saint Augustine* (ET New York 1968).
47. F. van der Meer, *Augustine de Zielsorger* (Utrecht 1947); ET *Augustine the Bishop* (London 1961).
48. *Oratio 2,* translated as 'In defence of his Flight to Pontus, and his Return,

after his Ordination to the Priesthood, with an Exposition of the Character of the Priestly Office', in C.G. Browne and J.E. Swallow (trs.), *Selection Orations of S. Gregory Nazianzen*, = *Nicene and Post-Nicene Fathers* N.S. 7 (Oxford-New York 1894), pp. 204-227.

49. *De officiis* may be found in English as 'Three Books on the Duties of the Clergy', in H. de Romestin, (tr. *Some of the Principal Works of St Ambrose* = *Nicene and Post-Nicene Fathers* N.S. 10 (Oxford-New York 1896), pp. 1-90.

50. *De Sacerdotio* II. 1. The English translation used is that of W.A. Jurgens, *The Priesthood. A Translation of the 'Peri Hierosynes' of S. John Chrysostom* (New York 1955).

51. Ibid., II.4.

52. Ibid., IV.5.

53. Ibid., VI.4.

54. Ezekiel 33: 2, 6, at *De Sacerdotio* VI.1.

55. J. Richards, *Consul of God, The Life and Times of Gregory the Great* (London 1980), p. 54.

56. Ezekiel 33: 2, 6, op. cit. VI.10.

57. F. H. Dudden, *Gregory the Great. His Place in History and Thought* (London 1905), II.

58. *Regula pastoralis* II.1. A convenient English version is H. Davis S.J. (tr.), *St Gregory the Great, Pastoral Care* (Westminster, Maryland and London 1950), = *Ancient Christian Writers* No.11.

Chapter 3: The Medieval Theology of Order

1. L. Saltet, *Les réordinations* (Paris 1907), p. 211.

2. Bede, *Ecclesiastical History of the English People*, IV. 2 (B. Colgrave and R.A.B. Mynors (eds.), Oxford 1969), pp. 334-335.

3. *Prescription* 26, cited L. Saltet, *Les réordinations*, op. cit., p. 89.

4. See J. Tixeront, *L'Ordre et les ordinations. Etude de théologie historique* (Paris 1925), pp. 417-418.

5. L. Saltet, *Les réordinations*, op. cit. pp. 101 ff.

6. Hincmar of Rheims, *De excommunicatis vitandis, de reconciliatione lapsorum et de fontibus juris ecclesiastici*, P. L. 148, col. 1181.

7. *Liber gratissimus*, P. L. 145, col. 90.

8. *Adversus simoniacos*, P. L. 143, col. 1005.

9. L. Saltet, *Les réordinations*, op. cit., p. 211.

10. A. Michel, 'Ordre', art. cit., col. 1289.

11. Cited from Bernold's *De sacramentis excommunicatorum*, P. L. 148, col. 1061.

12. A. Michel, 'Ordre', art. cit., cols. 1290-1291.

13. Ibid., col. 1293.

14. Ibid., cols. 1296-1297.

15. For the teaching of Rufinus' *Summa Decreti*, see ibid., cols. 1295-1296.

16. D.N. Power, OMI, *Ministers of Christ and his Church. The Theology of the Priesthood* (London 1969), p. 99.

17. Ibid., p. 92.
18. *Liber officialis* II. 13, 1.
19. *Capitula ad presbyteros parochiae suae* I; P. L. 105, col. 193.
20. D. N. Power, OMI, *Ministers of Christ and his Church,* op. cit., p. 96, cf. B. Botte, OSB, 'Imitatio', Alma 16 (1942), pp. 148–154.
21. *De clericorum institutione* I. 6: P. L. 107, col. 302.
22. Honorius of Autun, *Gemma animae* I. 181: P. L. 172, col. 599: Amalarius of Metz, *De ecclesiasticis officiis* II. 13: P. L. 105, col. 1090.
23. D.N. Power, OMI, *Ministers of Christ and his Church,* op. cit., p. 98.
24. *De sacramentis* II. 5: P. L. 176, col. 423.
25. *Liber Sententiarum* IV., dist. 24–25.
26. A.O. Lovejoy, *The Great Chain of Being. A Study of the History of an Idea* (New York 1960), see also P.G. Kuntz, 'Order', *New Catholic Encyclopaedia* 10, pp. 720–723.
27. *In quartum librum Sententiarum* dist. 24, a. 2, q. 1; *Summa contra Gentiles* IV. 74.
28. *In quartum librum Sententiarum,* dist. 24, pars 1, a. 2, q.2.
29. A. Michel, 'Ordre', art. cit., col. 1305.
30. Ibid., col. 1305, with reference to: Thomas, *Summa Theologiae,* Suppl., q. 36, a. 8, ad ii; Bonaventure, *In quartum librum Sententiarum,* dist. 25, a. 2, q. iv.
31. Ibid., dist. 24, pars 1, a. 2, q. iii.
32. A. Michel, 'Ordre', art. cit., cols. 1306–1307.
33. *De bono conjugali* 21: the consecration which ordination brings about is *ordinis Ecclesiae signaculum.*
34. J. Galot, SJ, *La Nature du caractère sacramentel. Etude de théologie médiévale* (Gembloux 1956), p. 224.
35. Ibid., p. 227.
36. Ibid., pp. 228–229.
37. Ibid., pp. 229–230.
38. Thomas Aquinas, *Summa Theologiae* IIIa, q.63, a.3., *corpus.*
39. W. Kasper, 'Ministry in the Church: Taking Issue with Edward Schillebeeckx', *Communio* X. 2 (summer 1983), pp. 185–195, and here at p. 189.
40. Ibid. In this connection, it is not difficult to see why another contemporary theologian has declared that, for certain radical critics of the Catholic tradition, 'the de-mystification of character must justify that of the priesthood, reduced to a simple function', J. Galot, SJ, 'Le Caractère sacerdotal', in J. Hernandez, OSA, et al., *Teologia del Sacerdocio: 3. El Sacerdote ministro de la Iglesia* (Burgos 1971), pp. 115–131, and here at p. 117.
41. Thomas Aquinas, *Summa Theologiae* IIIa, q.63, a.2, *corpus.*
42. D. N. Power, OMI, *Ministers of Christ and his Church,* op. cit., pp. 119–120; Father Power's account synthesises *Summa Theologiae* IIIa Pars, q. 67, a. 2; q. 82, a. 1, with ibid., IIa IIae, q. 184, a. 5, and *Summa contra Gentiles* IV. 76.
43. For Thomas on the presbyter's power of the keys, see idem., *Commentarium in Sententiarum libros,* IV. dist. 18, q. 1, a. i.

44. *Reportatio* IV. 10.
45. Thomas: *Summa Theologiae,* Suppl., q. 37, a. 2, ad ii; Bonaventure, *In quartum librum Sententiarum,* dist. 24, pars II, q. 1, ad iii.
46. A. Michel, 'Ordre', art. cit., col. 1308.
47. Ibid., col. 1309.
48. Ibid., col. 1307.
49. For the abusive papal 'dispensations', see J. Beyer, 'Nature et position du Sacerdoce', *Nouvelle Revue Théologique* 76 (1954), pp. 364-376.
50. J. H. Martin, OP, 'The Injustice of Not Ordaining Women: A Problem for Mediaeval Theologians', *Theological Studies* 48, 2 (June 1987), pp. 303-316.
51. R. P. Stenger, 'The Episcopacy as an Ordo according to the Mediaeval Canonists', *Mediaeval Studies* 29 (1967), pp. 67-112.

Chapter 4: The Reformers and the Council of Trent

1. The often praiseworthy original impulse of such groups seeking an evangelical life-style should not, however, be overlooked: see G. Leff, *Heresy in the Later Middle Ages. The Relation of Heterodoxy to Dissent c.1250-c.1450* (Manchester 1967), pp. 2-3. On the general background of an 'age of unrest' see R.W. Southern, *Western Society and the Church in the Middle Ages* (Harmondsworth 1970) pp. 44-52.
2. On Hussitism, see H. Kaminsky, *A History of the Hussite Revolution* (Berkeley-Los Angeles 1967).
3. For the Fraticelli, see G. Leff, *Heresy in the Later Middle Ages,* op. cit., pp. 53-255. The term covers a number of 'Dissident Franciscans, some derived from the fugitive Anconan and Tuscan Spirituals under Henry of Ceva, others descended from the followers of Michael of Cesena. The first, who, after being expelled from Sicily settled in southern Italy and the region of the Romagna, are sometimes known as the *Fraticelli de paupere vita;* the second as the *Fraticelli de opinione.* They had nothing in common save a common hostility to John XXII and his successors, nor did they stand for much more in themselves', ibid., p. 231. However, some of the Fraticelli anticipated Wyclif in holding that, e.g., a priest in mortal sin could not administer the sacraments, and that a priest who fell into heretical opinions lost his sacramental powers, ibid., p. 232. See also, D.L. Douie, *The Nature and the Effect of the Heresy of the Fraticelli* (Manchester, 1932).
4. S. Runciman, *The Mediaeval Manichee* (Cambridge 1947).
5. Cf. G. Leff, *Heresy in the Later Middle Ages,* op. cit., p. 29: 'The dualist tendencies of Catharism were to be found among the Waldensians until the end of the fourteenth century....'.
6. Ibid., p. 31.
7. Ibid. pp. 308-407. Note the idea that the perfect man does not need a priest: pp. 313; 327.
8. Ibid. p. 194.
9. Ibid. pp. 494-558.

10. *Trialogus* IV. 15.
11. On Hus and his doctrine, see M. Spinka, *John Hus. A Biography* (Princeton 1968); idem., *John Hus' Concept of the Church* (Princeton 1966);
12. Denzinger-Schönmetzer 1262.
13. Cited in J. Lécuyer, CSSp, *What is a Priest?*, op. cit.
14. D. Martin Luthers *Werke* 6 (Weimar 1888), pp. 560-567.
15. W. Stein, *Das kirchliche Amt bei Luther* (Wiesbaden 1974), p. 200. See also J. Pelikan, *Spirit versus Structure. Luther and the Institutions of the Church* (New York 1968).
16. *P. Melanthonis Opera quae supersunt omnia* V (Halle 1838), pp. 210-211, = *Letter* 2786, 'Iudicium de impositione manuum'.
17. Ibid. XXI (Braunschweig 1854), pp. 470-471.
18. See especially his comments on articles XIV and XXVIII of the *Augustana* in the *Apologia pro Confessione Augustana*, ibid. XXVII (Braunschweig 1859), p. 288, and pp. 310-315.
19. Schmalkaldic Articles III. 10. In the tractate *De potestate et primatu papae* appended to the Articles, the authors, citing Jerome in particular, insist, however, that the distinction between presbyter and bishop is of merely human making.
20. *Institutes* IV. 19, 22-33.
21. Cf. the discussion of Calvin's position by Max Thurian in idem., *Priesthood and Ministry. Ecumenical Research* (ET London 1983), where the author argues that Calvin's denial of the *name* sacrament to ordination derived from his stipulation that only sacraments conferred on all Christians may be so called. He concludes that, in later Calvinism, 'the sacramental conception of ordination was allowed to be weakened', p. 156. See on the whole subject, A. Ganoczy, *Calvin, théologien de l'Eglise et du ministère* (Paris 1964).
22. See W.P. Stephens, *The Theology of Huldrych Zwingli* (Oxford 1986).
23. D.C. Steinmetz, 'Luther and Calvin on Church and Tradition', in idem., *Luther in Context* (Bloomington, Indiana, 1986), pp. 96-97.
24. Board for Mission and Unity of the Church of England, *The Priesthood of the Ordained Ministry* (London 1986), p. 57.
25. F. Clark SJ, *Anglican Orders and Defect of Intention* (London 1956), p. 161.
26. *The Defence of the Priesthood* (ET London 1935), prologue, p. 3.
27. Ibid. 2; pp. 4-5.
28. The fullest account of Mensing's life and work is in N. Paulus, *Die deutschen Dominikaner im Kampfe gegen Luther* (Freiburg 1903), pp. 16-47. The full Latin titles are: *De sacerdotio ecclesiae Christi catholicae: oratio latina: habita ad clerum Parthenopolitanum: adversus Mart. Lutheri dogmata, praesertim libello suo infando, de abroganda missa, malesuado demone prodita*, and *Examen Scripturarum atque argumentorum: quae adversus sacerdotium ecclesiae: libello de abrogando Missa, per M. Lutherum sunt adducta*. They were published in a more convenient double format by J. Host von Romberg as *M. Joannis Mensingi Theologi de Ecclesia Christi sacerdotio Libri duo*, with additions, in Cologne in 1532, and republished by T. Mensing in Cologne in 1682.

29. Mention should be made here, nonetheless, of Pope Leo X's anticipation of that consensus, in his bull *Exsurge Domine*, of 1520, which maintained, against Luther, the necessary role of the ministerial priesthood in the forgiveness of grave post-baptismal sin, seeing Church Penance as a genuine sacrament confided to the apostolic ministry in the promise of Christ to the Twelve that whose sins they forgave on earth, would be deemed forgiven in heaven, see D-S, 1451-1465; 1667-1693.

30. Cited in A. Michel, 'Ordre', art. cit., cols. 1349-1350.

31. For the text, see, most conveniently, D-S 1763-1770

32. J. Waterworth, *The Canons and Decrees of the Council of Trent* (London 1848), p. 27.

33. Ibid., p. 211.

34. A. Gouze, OP, 'L'importance de la liturgie', in *Dieu est amour. Saint Dominique et l'Ordre des Prêcheurs* (Paris 1984), p. 43.

35. J. Waterworth, *The Canons and Decrees of the Council of Trent,* op. cit., p. 214.

36. *Catechismus romanus, ex decreto Sacrosancti Concilii Tridentini, jussu Pii V, Pontificis maximi, editus* (Rome 1566); ET *The Catechism of the Council of Trent,* translated into English, with Notes, by T.A. Buckley (London 1852)

37. Ibid., II.7, 2

38. Ibid., II.7, 5

39. For the canons of Trent, see D-S 1771-1778 op. cit.

40. G. Bardy et al., *Prêtres d'hier et d'aujourd'hui* (Paris 1954), p. 197.

41. See J. Bergin, *Cardinal de la Rochefoucauld. Leadership and Reform in the French Church* (New Haven and London 1987), p. 99; and for surveys, the pioneering H. Jedin, 'Das Bischofsideal der katholischen Reformation', in idem., *Kirche des Glaubens, Kirche der Geschichte. Gesammelte Aufsätze* (Freiburg 1966) and B. M. Bosatra, 'Ancora sul "vescovo ideale" della riforma cattolica. I lineamenti del pastore tridentino-borromaico', *Scuola Cattolica* 112 (1984), pp. 517-579.

42. H. Jedin, *Carlo Borromeo* (Rome 1971), pp. 12-13. Bartholomew would later give his ideas written form in his *Stimulus pastorum* (Paris 1583).

43. J.A. O'Donoghue, *Tridentine Seminary Legislation: its Sources and its Formation* (Louvain 1957).

44. *Epistola 63.*

45. T.J. van Bavel, *The Rule of St Augustine: Introduction and Commentary* (ET London 1984); G. Lawless, OSA, *Augustine of Hippo and his Monastic Rule* (Oxford 1987).

46. H. Rackham, *Early Statutes of Christ's College, Cambridge* (Cambridge 1927), p. 103.

47. J.A. O'Donoghue, op. cit., pp. 89-120.

48. M.H. Vicaire, OP, in G. Bardy et al., *Prêtres d'hier et d'aujourd'hui,* op. cit., p. 209.

49. H. Jedin, 'Le Concile de Trente a-t-il formé l'image-modèle du prêtre?', in J. Coppens (ed.), *Sacerdoce et célibat. Etudes doctrinales et historiques* (Louvain 1970). pp. 11-31.

50. For the quality of Eucharistic theology they had inherited, see the spirited defence of late medieval teaching in F. Clark, SJ, *Eucharistic Sacrifice and the Reformation* (London 1960).

Chapter 5: From the Council of Trent to the Catholic Revival

1. Affirmed by Bellarmine against the view of Domingo Soto that the *porrectio instrumentorum* suffices: he based his position on the evidence of Scripture, the ancient Councils, the Fathers and the practice of the Greek church in his own day; so, his *De ordine* 9.
2. Ibid., 5.
3. Pétau devoted the first two books of the *De ecclesiastica hierarchia* to setting forth the historical evidence for this important thesis, to which he returned in the *Dissertationum ecclesiasticarum libri duo,* insisting that the episcopate is not only a distinct 'dignity' from the presbyterate, but a different 'power'.
4. In his *Commentarius de sacris Ecclesiae ordinationibus* (Paris 1655).
5. Morin argued that a given local church, or even individual bishop, may be more exigent in what it regards as the necessary matter of the sacrament, such that, as with marriage or penance, if certain things are not carried out, this may, in some circumstances, render the attempt to celebrate the sacrament null. Morin intended here to commend, and justify, the re-ordination of heretical ministers, such as those from the churches of the Reform.
6. Mabillon specialised in the *Ordines romani;* Edmond Martène, of the same Congregation, ranged more widely in his *De antiquis Ecclesiae ritibus* (Rouen 1700). Goar specialised in the Byzantine liturgy, studied in his *Euchologion sive rituale Graecorum* (Paris 1647).
7. *Instruction sur les états d'oraison* vi.
8. S. Ryan, 'Episcopal Consecration: the Fulness of Order', *Irish Theological Quarterly* XXXII. 4 (October 1965), p. 303.
9. F. Hallier, *De sacris electionibus et ordinationibus, ex antiquo et novo Ecclesiae usu,* (Rome 1739-1740).
10. A. de Molina, *Instrucciones de sacerdotes* (Burgos 1608).
11. A. Michel, 'Ordre', art, cit., col. 1375.
12. E. A. Walsh, *The Priesthood in the Writings of the French School: Bérulle, De Condren, Olier* (Washington 1949).
13. J. Bergin, *Cardinal de la Rochefoucauld, Leadership and Reform in the French Church,* op. cit., pp. 106-107. The internal citation is from J. Choné, 'La Spiritualité sacerdotale', *XVII Siècle* 62-3 (1964), p. 123; that from the *Estat* is at pp. 379-380.
14. For Bérulle, see especially J. Dagens, *Bérulle et les origines de la restauration catholique 1575-1611* (Paris 1952); M. Dupuy, *Bérulle et le sacerdoce* (Paris 1969).
15. Ibid., p. 70.
16. Ibid., p. 75.
17. Ibid., p. 104.

18. J. Dagens (ed.), *Correspondance du Cardinal Pierre de Bérulle* (Paris-Louvain 1937-1939), p. 138.
19. R. Taveneau, *Le Catholicisme dans la France classique 1610-1715* (Paris 1980); M. Arneth, *Das Ringen um Geist und Form der Priesterbildung im Säkularklerus des 17. Jahrhunderts* (Würzburg 1970).
20. G. M. Hopkins' translation: 'Oratio patris Condren: O Jesu vivens in Maria', in W. H. Gardner and N. H. Mackenzie (ed.), *The Poems of Gerard Manley Hopkins* (London 1967), pp. 212-213.
21. B. Nodet, *Jean-Marie Vianney, Curé d'Ars: sa pensée, son coeur* (Le Puy 1958); *Pope John Paul II, The Ideal of the Priesthood, in the Spirit of the Curé d'Ars* (Preston, n.d.).
22. Information supplied by the Revd Dr Dermot Fenlon of St Mary's College, Oscott.
23. For his life, see A. Wilson, *The Life of Bishop Hedley* (London 1930); for a bibliography of his writings, G. Sitwell, 'Hedley (John Cuthbert)', *Dictionnaire de Spiritualité* t.7 (Paris 1968), cols. 132-133.
24. R. Gray, *Cardinal Manning. A Biography* (London 1985).
25. C.S. Dessain, *John Henry Newman* (London 1971); I. Ker, *John Henry Newman. A Biography* (Oxford 1989); and on the theme here singled out, G.W. Rutler, *Priests of the Gospel: a Comparison of the Second Vatican Council and John Henry Cardinal Newman on the Priest as a Preacher* (Rome 1982).
26. J.C. Hedley, *Lex Levitarum, or Preparation for the Cure of Souls* (Westminster 1906).
27. Cited from I. Schück, *Handbuch der Pastoraltheologie* (Innsbrück 1893), p. 16, at *Lex Levitarum*, op. cit., pp. 4-5.
28. Ibid., p. 7.
29. Ibid., pp. 7-8.
30. Ibid., p. 12.
31. Ibid., pp. 15-16.
32. Ibid., p. 23
33. Ibid., p. 27
34. Ibid., p. 44
35. Ibid., p. 75
36. Ibid., p. 77.
37. H. E. Manning, *The Eternal Priesthood* (London 1883).
38. Ibid., p. 10.
39. Ibid., p. 11.
40. J. Galot, SJ, *La Nature du caractère sacramentel*, op. cit., p. 158; cf. Bonaventure, *In quartum librum Sententiarum*. d. vi, p. 1, q. 2, ad ii.
41. H. E. Manning, *The Eternal Priesthood*, op. cit., p. 44.
42. Ibid., p. 199.
43. Ibid., p. 223.
44. Ibid., pp. 223-224.
45. G.W. Rutler, *Priests of the Gospel*, op. cit., p. 102.
46. Ibid., p. 94.
47. See P. Murray (ed.), *Newman the Oratorian. His Unpublished Oratory Papers* (Dublin 1969), p. 161.

48. G. W. Rutler, *Priests of the Gospel,* op. cit., pp. 200-201. The author arrives at this statement by applying Newman's teaching on the threefold *munus* of the apostolic ministry in such passages as *Sermons Bearing on Subjects of the Day* (London 1843; 1902), p. 55, to Rutler's belief that Newman considered preaching as the *primum officium* of the priest — thus anticipating the Second Vatican Council's extension to the presbyter, in *Presbyterorum Ordinis* 4, of what Trent had maintained of the bishop.

Chapter 6: From the Catholic Revival to the Second Vatican Council

1. For an excellent overview, though in a comparatively inaccessible language, see P. E. Persson, *Kyrkans ämbete som Kristus-representation. En kritisk analys av nyare ämbetsteologi* (Lund 1961).
2. Ibid., p. 16.
3. C. Journet, *L'Eglise du Verbe incarné* (Paris 1951-1969).
4. Ibid., I. p. 32.
5. J.H. Newman, 'The Christian Ministry', in *Parochial and Plain Sermons,* op. cit., II. pp. 303-304.
6. Thus, in *Sacramentum ordinis,* the Germanic legal form of the *traditio instrumentorum,* with the mandate to offer sacrifice, which, as the common teaching of late medieval theologians, had been used, in the aftermath of the Council of Florence, to draw up an account of the Church's sacramental teaching for reconciled Armenian Christians (the *Decretum pro Armeniis*), was relegated to secondary significance in comparison with the practice of the ancient Church. The reconstitution of the primary gesture of ordination was at the same time a recovery of a more fully pneumatological, and not simply christological account of Order — since the gesture of the laying on of hands is of its nature an *epiklêsis,* a plea for the descent of the Spirit. For the text, see *Acta Apostolicae Sedis* 40 (1948), pp. 5-7. Some theologians, however, hold that the Church, using the power to make more specific the sacramental symbolism (or to make conditions affecting validity) had so added the *traditio instrumentorum* that it formed a part of the matter required for validity (in that period). Pius XII's document makes careful allowance for this view.
7. The text of *Mediator Dei* is found in idem., 39 (1947), pp. 521-595. The section bearing on the relation of the ministerial priest to Christ as Head is at p. 538.
8. On this, see K.J. Becker, 'Der Unterschied von Bischof und Priester im Weihedekret des Konzils von Trient und nach der Kirchenkonstitution des II Vatikanischen Konzils', in K. Rahner (ed.), *Zum Problem Unfehlbarkeit. Antworten auf die Anfrage von Hans Küng* (Freiburg 1971), pp. 291-308.
9. J. Lécuyer, *Le Sacerdoce dans le mystère du Christ* (Paris 1957), pp. 409-410.
10. *Lumen Gentium* 20.
11. Ibid., 19.
12. Ibid., 22.

13. 'Nota explicativa praevia', in *Acta Synodalia Sacrosancti Concilii Oecumenici Vaticani Secundi,* III, 8 (Vatican City 1976), p. 11.
14. J. Galot, SJ, *Theology of the Priesthood* (ET San Francisco 1984), p. 186.
15. *Lumen Gentium* 28.
16. Ibid. 29; *Constitutions of the Egyptian Church* III. 2.
17. *Lumen Gentium* 28.
18. German Catholic authors produced here some monumental studies; see especially: H. Krimm (ed.), *Das diakonische Amt der Kirche* (Stuttgart 1953; 1965); idem. (ed.), *Quellen zur Geschichte der Diakonie* (Stuttgart 1960-1964); H. Rahner, SJ-H. Vorgrimler (eds.), *Diaconia in Christo. Über die Erneuerung des Diakonates* (Freiburg 1962), with full bibliography.
19. D.N. Power, OMI, *Ministers of Christ and his Church. The Theology of the Priesthood* (London 1969), p. 109.
20. Ibid., p. 113.
21. *Presbyterorum ordinis* 2.
22. Ibid., 4.
23. Ibid., 5.
24. Ibid., 6.
25. Ibid., 2.
26. Ibid., cf. 5.
27. Ibid., 5.
28. Ibid., 12, citing Hebrews 7:26.
29. *Presbyterorum ordinis* 18, with a reference to Romans 8:15.
30. *Presbyterorum ordinis* 1.
31. Ibid. 2, with a reference, via *Lumen Gentium* 10, to Pius XII's remarks on the differentiation of the universal and ministerial priesthood in the encyclical *Mediator Dei* of 20 November 1947, as also in the allocution *Magnificate Dominum* of 2 November 1954.
32. For a full discussion of the document, see J. Frisque, 'Le décret *Presbyterorum ordinis:* histoire et commentaire', in J. Frisque - Y. Congar (eds.), *Les Prêtres: Décrets 'Presbyterorum ordinis' et 'Optatam totius'* (Paris 1968).

Conclusion

1. For a fuller exploration of the factors operative in this crisis, see B. Kloppenburg, OFM, *The Priest. Living Instrument and Minister of Christ the Eternal Priest* (ET Chicago 1974), pp. 1-26.
2. It is true that there are cases where we bestow the presbyterate on individuals who will not be able to realise this unity in its completeness — for example on priests in enclosed monasteries. But we realise that these are 'hard cases' which have to be specially justified. As with the parallel case of those bishops who do not exemplify the full pattern of the episcopate, 'auxiliary' bishops, including the auxiliaries of the pope in the *curia romana,* their existence is not self-evidently right, but they can nevertheless be argued for.

Appendix: Two disputed questions

1. The ordination of women

1. For this text, see A. von Harnack, *Die Quellen der sogenannten apostolischen Kirchenordnung* (Leipzig 1886), p. 28; cf. J. Owen, *Sources of the Apostolic Canons* (London 1895), p. 24; = ET of the former.
2. E.L. Mascall, 'Some Basic Considerations', in P. Moore (ed.), *Man, Woman, and Priesthood* (London 1978), pp. 9-26, and here at p. 23.
3. *Commonitorium primum* 2, 3 (P.L. 50, 640).
4. K. Ware, 'Man, Woman and the Priesthood of Christ', in T. Hopko (ed.), *Women and the Priesthood* (Crestwood, New York, 1983), pp. 9-38, and here at p. 12.
5. J.-J. Allmen, cited in ibid., pp. 13-14.
6. J. H. Newman, *An Essay on the Development of Christian Doctrine* (London 1845; 1974), pp. 133-136.
7. *Epistola* 63.
8. *Homilia* 123.
9. *Seven Chapters against the Iconoclasts* 4.
10. M. Aghiorgoussis, *Women Priests?* (Brookline, Massachusetts 1976), p. 5.
11. R. W. Jenson, *The Triune Identity. God according to the Gospel* (Philadelphia 1982), pp. 15-16.
12. It may be relevant to note that the first offshoot from the Great Church to practice the ordination of women was Montanism — whose peculiar doctrine of the incarnate Paraclete involved precisely an illicit abrogation of the infinite qualitative difference between Creator and creature.
13. See *De veritate* X.13; and on this whole area, T.C. O'Brien, 'Names Proper to the Divine Person, in idem., *St Thomas Aquinas, Summa Theologiae*, Vol. 7. *Father, Son and Holy Ghost (Ia, 33-43)*, (London 1976), pp. 239-251.
14. See J. A. Little, 'Sexual Equality in the Church: a Theological Resolution to the Anthropological Dilemma', *Heythrop Journal* XXVIII (1987), pp. 165-178.
15. *Didascalia Apostolorum*, ed. R. H. Connolly (Oxford 1929), 25.
16. S. Terrien, *Till the Heart Sings. A Biblical Theology of Manhood and Womanhood* (Philadelphia 1985).
17. O. Clément, cited E. L. Mascall, 'Some Basic Considerations', art. cit., p. 20.
18. *Christifideles laici* (= Post-Synodal Apostolic Exhortation of John Paul II on the Vocation and Mission of the Laity in the Church and in the World), 23.
19. P. Hebblethwaite, *In the Vatican* (Oxford 1987), p. 175.
20. J. Daniélou, SJ, *The Ministry of Women in the Early Church* (London 1961), pp. 14-31; cf. A.G. Martimort, *Les Diaconesses. Etude historique* (Rome 1982).
21. Ibid., p. 254.
22. R. J. Barratt, 'Rediscovering the diaconate', *Priests and People* 2, 9 (November 1988), p. 352, with reference to the invoking of the examples

of Miriam, Deborah and Anna in *Apostolic Constitutions* VIII. 20.
23. M.-J. Aubert, *Des femmes diacres? Un nouveau chemin pour l'Eglise* (Paris 1987).

2. Priesthood and celibacy

24. R. Cholij, 'Celibacy: A Tradition of the Eastern Churches', *Priests and People* (July/August 1988), II. 6., pp. 208-221, and here at p. 208. This article constitutes a convenient summary, though without footnoting, of the much more extended version of his thesis found as 'Married Clergy and Ecclesiastical Continence in Light of the Council *in Trullo* (691), in *Annuarium Historiae Conciliorum* 19, 1 (1987), pp. 71-230; and ibid., 2 (1987), pp. 241-299. This study is now more readily accessible as *Clerical Celibacy in East and West* (Leominster 1989).
25. See A. M. Stickler, 'The evolution of the discipline of celibacy in the Western Church from the end of the patristic era to the Council of Trent', in J. Coppens (ed.), *Priesthood and Celibacy* (ET Milan-Rome 1971), pp. 503-598.
26. Socrates, *Historia ecclesiastica*, 1, 11; Sozomen, *Historia ecclesiastica*, 1, 23.
27. C. Cochini, SJ, *Origines apostoliques du célibat sacerdotal* (Paris 1981).
28. Cited from the *Codex canonum Ecclesiae Africanae* of 419 in P.P. Joannou, *Discipline générale antique* (IIe-IXe siècle), I. 2. *Les canons des synodes particuliers* (Grottaferrata 1962), pp. 216-217.
29. R. Cholij, 'Celibacy...', art. cit., p. 221.
30. H. Crouzel, 'Celibacy and Ecclesiastical Continence in the Early Church: the Motives Involved', in J. Coppens (ed.), *Priesthood and Celibacy*, op. cit., pp. 457-458.
31. Cited in R. Gryson, *Les Origines du célibat ecclésiastique. Du premier au septième siècle* (Bembloux 1970), p. 61.
32. Cited in P. P. Joannou, *Discipline générale antique*, op. cit., I. 1. *Les canons des conciles oecuméniques*, pp. 140-143.
33. R. Cholij, 'Married Clergy and Ecclesiastical Continence...', art. cit., p. 244.
34. Idem., 'Celibacy', art. cit., p. 221.
35. E. Schillebeeckx, *Clerical Celibacy under Fire* (ET London 1968), p. 25.
36. Ibid., p. 23, citing Matthew 19:12.
37. H. Crouzel, 'Celibacy and Ecclesiastical Continence in the Early Church', art. cit., pp. 467-488.
38. The letter is found at *Acta Apostolicae Sedis* 59 (1967), pp. 657-697, and here at p. 665.
39. A. Stickler, 'La continenza dei diaconi specialmente nel primo millenio della Chiesa', *Salesianum* 26 (1964), pp. 275-302.
40. R.E. Brown, SS, *Priest and Bishop*, op. cit., p. 26.
41. J.M. Lustiger, *Dare to Believe* (ET New York 1986), p. 209.
42. Archbishop Stafford, 'The Mystery of the Priestly Vocation', *Origins* 18. 22 (10 November 1988), citing Ephesians 5:22-33.

Select Bibliography

General histories

'Ordre', *Dictionnaire de Théologie Catholique* XI. 2 (Paris 1932) cols. 1193-1405.

B. Cooke, *Ministry to Word and Sacraments. History and Theology* (Philadelphia 1976).

J. Delormé (ed), *The Sacrament of Holy Orders* (ET Collegeville 1962).

D. N. Power, OMI, *Ministers of Christ and his Church. The Theology of the Priesthood* (London 1969).

B. Bardy et al., *Prêtres d'hier et d'aujourd'hui* (Paris 1954).

L. Ott, *Das Weihesakrament* (Freiburg 1969, = *Handbuch der Dogmengeschichte* IV. 5).

Documents of the Magisterium

K. J. Becker, *Der priesterliche Dienst II. Wesen und Vollmacht des Priestertums nach dem Lehramt,* = *Quaestiones disputatae* 47 (Freiburg 1970).

K. Rahner (ed.), *The Teaching of the Catholic Church as Contained in her Documents* (Cork 1966), pp. 339-350.

Inter insigniores = SCDF, Declaration on the Question of the Admission of Women to the Ministerial Priesthood, 1976. CTS Do 493.

Sacerdotium ministeriale = SCDF, Letter to the Bishops of the Catholic Church on Certain Questions Concerning the Minister of the Eucharist, 1983. CTS Do 550.

Commission Théologique Internationale (Pontifical International Theological Commission), *Le sacerdoce catholique,* 1970.

Idem., *L'apostolicité de l'Eglise et la succession apostolique,* 1973. ET *Catholic Teaching on Apostolic Succession,* CTS Do 466.

The New Testament

A. M. Farrer, 'The Ministry in the New Testament', in K. E. Kirk (ed.), *The Apostolic Ministry* (London 1946), pp. 113-182 (Anglican).

J. Colson, *Ministère de Jésus Christ et le sacerdoce de l'évangile* (Paris 1966).

P. Grelot, *Le ministère de la nouvelle alliance* (Paris 1967).

A. Lemaire (ed.), *Les ministères aux origines de l'Eglise* (Paris 1971: NB written from 'contestatory' standpoint).

A. Vanhoye, *Old Testament Priests, New Testament Priests* (ET Stillwater, Massachusetts 1982).

A. Feuillet, *The Priesthood of Christ and his Ministers* (ET New York 1975).

R. E. Brown, *Priest and Bishop. Biblical Reflections* (London 1971)

The 'Schillebeeckx debate'

E. Schillebeeckx, *Ministry. A Case for Change* (London 1981) *The Church with a Human Face. A New and Expanded Theology of Ministry* (London 1985).

P. Grelot, *Eglise et ministères. Pour un dialogue critique avec Edward Schillebeeckx* (Paris 1983).

R. Malone (ed.), *Review of Contemporary Perspectives on Ministry* (Washington 1983): essays by Grelot, Kasper, Crouzel and Vanhoye 'critiqueing' Schillebeeckx.

Holy Order

The patristic period

G. Dix, 'The Ministry in the Early Church', in K. E. Kirk (ed.), *The Apostolic Ministry* (London 1946), pp. 183-204. (Anglo-Catholic).

R. J. Bastian, *Priesthood and Ministry,* = *Guide to the Fathers of the Church* 5 (Glen Rock, New Jersey 1969).

J. Colson, *Les fonctions ecclésiales aux deux premiers siècles* (Bruges 1956).

H. F. von Campenhausen, *Ecclesiastical Authority and Spiritual Power in the Church of the First Three Centuries* (ET London 1969).

Patristic texts

Augustine, *On Baptism, against the Donatists,* and *The Answer to Letters of Petilian,* in J. R. King (tr.), *Writings in Connection with the Donatist Controversy* (Edinburgh 1872).

Gregory Nazianzen, *Oration 2:* 'In Defence of his Flight to Pontus, and his Return, after his Ordination to the Priesthood, with an Exposition of the Character of the Priestly Office', in C. G. Browne and J. E. Swallow (trs.), *Selected Orations of S. Gregory Nazianzen,* = *Nicene and Post-Nicene Fathers* N.S. 7 (Oxford-New York 1894), pp. 204-227.

W. A. Jurgens, *The Priesthood. A Translation of the 'Peri Hierosynes' of S. John Chrysostom* (New York 1955).

Ambrose of Milan, 'Three Books on the Duties of the Clergy', in H. de Romestin (tr. *Some of the Principal Works of St Ambrose.* = *Nicene and Post-Nicene Fathers* N.S. 10 (Oxford-New York 1896), pp. 1-90.

H. Davis SJ (tr.), *St Gregory the Great, Pastoral Care* (Westminster, Maryland and London 1950), = *Ancient Christian Writers* No 11.

The medieval period

In addition to the general histories:

J. Périnelle, 'La doctrine de S. Thomas sur le sacrament de l'Ordre', *Recherches des Sciences Philosophiques et Théologiques* 1930.

A. McDevitt, 'The Episcopate as an Order and Sacrament on the Eve of the High Scholastic Period', *Franciscan Studies* 20 (1960), pp. 96-148.

S. Ryan, 'Episcopal Consecration: the Legacy of the Schoolmen', *Irish Theological Quarterly* 33, 1 (1966), pp. 3-38.

The Reformers and the Council of Trent

In addition to the general histories:

M. Spinka, *Advocates of Reform: from Wyclif to Erasmus* (London 1953).

R. E. Davies, *The Problem of Authority in the Continental Reformers* (London 1946).

D. C. Steinmetz, 'Luther and Calvin on Church and Tradition', in idem., *Luther in Context* (Bloomington, Indiana 1986), pp. 96-97.

W.P. Stephens, *The Theology of Huldrych Zwingli* (Oxford 1986).

John Fisher, *The Defence of the Priesthood* (ET London 1935).

From Trent to Vatican II
In addition to the general histories:
S. Ryan, 'Episcopal Consecration: Trent to Vatican II', *Irish Theological Quarterly* 33, 2 (1966), pp. 133-150.
Idem., 'Episcopal Consecration: the Rediscovery of the Epsicopate', ibid. 33, 3 (1966), pp. 208-241.
J. A. O'Donoghue, *Tridentine Seminary Legislation: its Sources and its Formation* (Louvain 1957).
E. A. Walsh, *The Priesthood in the Writings of the French School: Bérulle, De Condren, Olier* (Washington 1949).
H. E. Manning, *The Eternal Priesthood* (London 1883).
J. C. Hedley, *Lex levitarum, or Preparation for the Cure of Souls* (Westminster 1906).
H. Lennerz, *De sacramento ordinis* (Rome 1947).
H. Bouëssé, *Le sacerdoce chretien* (Bruges 1957).
J. Beyer, 'Nature et position du sacerdoce', *Nouvelle Revue Théologique* 76 (1954), pp. 356-373; 469-480.
R. E. Persson, *Kyrkans ämbete som Kristus-representation. En kritisk analys av nyare ämbetsteologi* (Lund 1971).
Pius XII, *Mediator Dei* (1947).
Idem., *Sacramentum Ordinis* (1947).

Documents of the Second Vatican Council:
Lumen Gentium
Christus Dominus
Presbyterorum Ordinis
Optatam totius
(also, Paul VI: *Sacrum diaconatus ordinem* (1967) and *Ad pascendum* (1972)

Contemporary Catholic theology of Order
B. D. Marlianges, *Clés pour une théologie du ministère* (Paris 1978).
M. Thurian, *Priesthood and Ministry. Ecumenical Research* (ET London 1983: Reformed, but Catholicising).
J. Galot, *Theology of the Priesthood* (ET San Francisco 1984).
T. F. O'Meara, *Theology of Ministry* (New York 1983).
G. H. Tavard, *A Theology for Ministry* (Wilmington, Delaware, 1983).
A. Vanhoye, 'Sacerdoce commun et sacerdoce ministériel: distinction et rapports', *Nouvelle Revue Théologique* 107 (1975), pp. 193-207.
G. Greshake, *Priester sein. Zur Theologie und Spiritualität des priestlichen Amtes* (Freiburg/Basle/Vienna 1982).
A. Favale, *Il ministero presbiterale. Aspetti dottrinali, pastorali, spirituali* (Rome 1989).

The ordination of women
T. Horko (ed.), *Women and the Priesthood* (Crestwood, New York, 1983): Eastern Orthodox.
P. Moore (ed.), *Man, Woman and Priesthood* (London 1978). mainly Anglican.
L. Bouyer, *Woman in the Church. With an epilogue by H. U. von Balthasar, and*

an essay by C. S. Lewis (San Francisco 1979).
D. Connell, 'Women Priests', *Briefing* 18. 13; = 24. 6. 1988.
J. Saward, *The Case against the Ordination of Women* (London 1975): Anglo-Catholic.
Idem., *Christ and his Bride* (London 1977).
J. Grelot, *Mission et ministère de la femme* (Paris 1973).
J. Hourcade, *La femme dans l'Eglise, Etude anthropologique et théologique des ministères feminins* (Paris 1983).

The presbyterate and celibacy
E. Schillebeeckx, *Clerical Celibacy Under Fire* (London 1968). .
A.-M. Charue et al., *Priesthood and Celibacy* (Milan, n.d.).
R. Gryson, *Les origines de célibat ecclésiastique du premier au septième siècle* (Paris 1970).
C. Cochini, *Origines apostoliques du célibat sacerdotal* (Paris 1981).
J. Coppens (ed.), *Sacerdoce et Célibat: Etudes historiques et théologiques* (Gembloux/Louvain 1971).
R. Cholij, *Clerical Celibacy in East and West* (Leominster 1989).

Index of names

A

Aaron 9, 71, 72
Aërius of Pontus 49
Aghiorgoussis, M. 148
Alexander of Hales 77
Alfred 65
Alger 69
Amalarius 71
Ambrose 52, 53, 55, 61-62, 63, 70, 105
Ambrosiaster 49, 50
Andronicus 15
Anthony of Molina 111
Antiochus of Mar Saba 148
Archaicus 25
Athanasius 51
Augustine 49, 64, 55-60, 67, 70, 105, 112

B

Barnabas 15, 16, 20, 21
Bartholomew de Martyribus 105
Basilides 35
Bede 72
Bellarmine, R. 104, 108
Benedict 64
Bergin, J. 111
Bernold 68-69
Bérulle, P. de 112-114
Biel, G. 79
Bonaventure 74, 75, 76, 122
Borromeo, C. 105, 107, 111
Bossuet, J.-B. 109
Brown, R. 10, 162
Bruno of Segni 69

C

Cajetan (saint) 111
Cranmer, J. 92-93, 95, 127
Ceadda 67

Charlemagne 65
Cholij, R. 156, 158-159
Cicero 62
Clement of Alexandria 157
Cochini, C. 156
Condren, C. de 114, 115
Congar, Y. 130
Constantine (anti-pope) 67
Cranmer, T. 95
Cyprian 37, 39, 41, 50, 52, 55, 59, 147

D

De la Rochefoucauld, F. 111
Denys, *see* Pseudo-Denys
Diocletian 43
Dix, G. 41, 44
Dub-dá-Crich 51
Dupuy, M. 113
Durandus, *see* William Durandus

E

Epiphanius 50, 157
Eusebius of Vercelli 105

F

Farrer, A. 29
Feuillet, A. 9, 11
Fisher, J. 96-97, 105
Fortunatus 25

G

Galot, J. 109
Gandulph 69-70
Goar, J. 109
Gouze, A. 102
Gratian 9, 159